William Pudsey

A political essay

Summary review of the kings and government of England since the Norman

conquest

William Pudsey

A political essay
Summary review of the kings and government of England since the Norman conquest

ISBN/EAN: 9783744739191

Printed in Europe, USA, Canada, Australia, Japan

Cover: Foto ©ninafisch / pixelio.de

More available books at **www.hansebooks.com**

A
Summary Review
OF THE

Kings and Government

OF

ENGLAND.

A POLITICAL ESSAY:

OR,

Summary Review

OF THE

Kings and Government

OF

ENGLAND

Since the *Norman* Conquest.

By *W. P——y.* Esq;.

Principis est Vertus maxima nosse suos. *Martial.*

All Precepts concerning Kings, are in effect comprehended in these Remembrances: Remember thou art a Man; Remember thou art God's Vicegerent. The one bridleth their Power, and the other their Will. Lord *Bacon*'s Remains.

LONDON:
Printed in the Year. 1698.

TO THE
READER.

'TIS said, Action is the Life of a Prince, Speculation of a Scholar: *If the first would give himself to Thinking somewhat more, and the latter to Action, perhaps it would not be amiss; they would Each of 'em discover some Defects in themselves, and Both be more Useful to the World. Be it how it will, however, I present you with my Thoughts, defective enough, as not being much seen in one or t'other; the Fruit of Idleness and turning over a few Books, for want of better Employment: They are some passing Observations on the Conduct of our Princes, who have managed the Scepter from the* Norman Conquest, *and Those that managed Them. I do not pretend hereby to limit the Descent of our Kings to*

To the READER.

that Line: I know the Learned derive their Pedigree from much higher Pretenſions, from I know not whence, even from Adam; and that will ſcarce ſatisfy; ſome will have them all the immediate Work of God; All Originals. I have not the Confidence to Dedicate this Iſſue, but only to a Random Patronage, if any one ſhall be ſo kind to give it a favourable Reception: Something like that with the Child left in the Temple-Cloyſters, with this Inſcription; Pray be exceeding kind to this Infant, as Related to Both Societies by Father and Mother's ſide. Some Authors who can bring in but the Name of a King, muſt intereſt Him in the Title, and think the Work preſently due to Majeſty, and preſume to Addreſs the Offspring to his Protection: But I do not think the Pretence of Duty doth ſufficiently Apologize for the Vanity and Ambition of it: Beſides, that Kings ſeldom read Books (they ſee with other Mens Eyes), and thoſe who did, have not much improv'd the Talent of Government to their

To the READER.

their Own, or the Nation's Advantage. I would have Address'd it to a Friend, (if I had any, as I should my self); yet I know not what Commission I have to venture a Friend's Reputation in my Bottom: Though after all, I must, in truth, beg leave to question, Whether there be any such thing as a True Friend, notwithstanding all the fine Harangues on that Subject: Not that, I hope, I have behaved my self so indifferently in my Conversation, as undeserving that Character; but I mean Regular Friendships are founded on adequate Considerations, and are generally too much upon the Square in mutual Expectation. Alas! I have nothing to leave a Friend, except it be Eudamidas's Legacy, a Wife and Children; and could I find a Charixenus or Aretheus, I should very willingly quit the World, and with greater Satisfaction, than to remain in it, unless it were only at the Instance of such a Friend, for his Service, and to pay him the Satisfaction of Gratitude in due Acknowledgments. But this is too extravagant an Ex-

To the READER.

Expectation; for *Eudamidas* had but One Daughter to bequeath between *Two Friends*, whereas I have enow to break *Friendship* it self; enow to set forth a decent *Parade* of Intercession for Mercy, if it should be my Misfortune to be convicted of a Capital Offence. Nevertheless, I have somewhat more particularly designed these short *Reflections* for the Entertainment of a particular Acquaintance or two; and that in a sort of Grateful *Return*, That as I have the Honour and Advantage of Improving by their Conversation, so I on my part might endeavour to contribute somewhat to their easier Information in some things, who have not Leisure, nor perhaps Inclination, to peruse larger Volumes, or to read over tedious Histories. 'Tis for this *Reason* especially, that I have contracted these *Remarks* into as narrow a *Room* as the Length and Variety of Matter will possibly bear; and *Brevity* is the only Commendation I expect; but this, I think, with some *Justness*; otherwise I am very little concerned at the Success, or with what Opinion I shall
be

To the READER.

be received in the World: I pretend but to Sketch, not to Draw exactly, not to a Finished Piece: Besides, I am sure there's no one can be more severe upon me, than I am upon my self; and there's scarce any body sharper-sighted to discover an Imperfection in a Child of my own, than the Father: And for this I have Authority. What you have, is but the Diversion of a long Vacation; one Summer's recollected Thoughts, drest up between a very ordinary Study and Garden, and without help from Conversation, as not having Opportunity to spend Time or Money any where abroad. I confess I might have made a more Elaborate Piece of it; I can't tell whether the better for that: But if the Subject of these Considerations seems to require a more serious and intent Application (as if any does, 'tis this in my Judgment), I hope it may put some other Person upon it, of better Qualifications, and of a greater Genius and Diligence this way. Not but that I my self have Leisure enough, God knows, and a little too much for a Man in my Circumstances:

But

To the READER.

But I must confess, for my part, as the World goes, I cannot think it Tanti: *For besides that a Man will hazard the Reputation of his own Understanding, in the Pretences of Reforming that of others, 'tis not in my Inclination to jade a Reader in a Journy of Paper and Ink, no more than my self: (The Drudgery of the Mind is of the worst sort), And 'twere well if some other Writers were of this Opinion, they would save a great deal of Trouble to others at least. If it be Objected, That I am not particular in my Citations; I confess it; I write an Essay, not a formal Treatise: But the Passages have been so beaten, and the Authorities so well known of late Years, that I conceive 'tis superfluous, and I needed not: However, I must aver they are Truths, and faithfully delivered, as well as my Memory will bear; which, I must confess, is treacherous enough: Yet I give you nothing but what I'm sure I my self have met with and received; and that any Man but moderately versed in Books, will easily discover and acknowledge: And in*

To the READER.

Arguments and *Authorities* which are not *Nice* or *Critical*, 'tis not of much Importance, or Material, to be so exact. Others, I suppose, will say, I touch things slightly. I agree it; I write not to those who are Strangers to Books and Reading, but to refresh their Memories, who, perhaps, may not have much better than my self; and to give Hints to those who are inclined to make larger Enquiries upon Occasion. It may serve to Admonish, if not to Inform; and may Divert, if it cannot Edify.

As to what relates to the *Justification* of this Government, it may be thought this comes out but poorly at this *Time of Day*, and is a sort of barbarous *Triumph* over the Silenc'd and Oppress'd: But those who know how early I was engaged in this Revolution another Way (as early almost as any Gentleman on this Side of the Water), cannot entertain such Thoughts of me: I can only say, I have not advanc'd one Expression upon that Consideration; and the Occasion given me now, was only

Reading

To the READER.

Reading over some Books which had been on both Sides Published, but not with Satisfactory Arguments to me, and not in so clear a Method on the Side of the Revolution, as I wish'd; and besides, I do not find that Men are less apt to Talk against the Government now, than they were Seven or Eight Years ago; and therefore I suppose this Publication may not be unseasonable, even under so Long and Prosperous a Success of this Establishment, which can never be made too Secure in the Hearts and Affections of the People.

Your Humble Servant,

W. P.

A Summary

A Summary Review

OF THE

KINGS and GOVERNMENT

OF

ENGLAND, &c.

'T IS somewhat wonderful, and I know not by what Fate it comes to pass, That those Nations which by Nature seem design'd to enjoy the most retired Repose and Tranquility, as not being by Situation involv'd in the common Hurlyburly of the World, should yet notwithstanding deny themselves that Happiness, as it seems, and run into equal Confusion and Trouble with the large Continents of Men. Whether it be that we ascribe too much, or too little, to the Powers above, and assume

to our selves too far in the Conduct of Human Affairs: Or whether, in truth, we are not permitted to establish that settled Peace and Pleasure here below, which Mortals in their Wisdom would fancy, and pretend to prescribe to themselves: Be it how it will; Is it not certain, that all States, Civil and Ecclesiastical too, when they have arriv'd to the Top of Grandeur, by a sort of Necessity, as it were, dissolve into Luxury, and by an unaccountable Weakness and Vanity dwindle into Disreputation, lose their Edge, and are disarm'd, till another Encroachment steps up, and takes the place? Not that all New Establishments and Reformations have been always for the better; but only to shew, that all sublunary things are subject to change.

However, That Government and some Form of Polity is necessary, cannot be disputed; though it may, what sort is: But admitting Monarchy to be the best Constitution, and with all the Compliments of Comparison and Advantages that the Church will have; for that doth not pretend that it is the *Only* Form approved by God, with exclusion to others; yet we see the best Scheme of this, whether Absolute, Limited, or Mixt, Hereditary, or Elective, hath never yet been capable to establish and secure it in Peace and Prosperity long; as it were to intimate, That even the wisest Scheme (if any such be) of Policy, will have its Defects; and all Foundations

dations of Government are planted in a changeable Soil, and are transform'd even in Notion, either through the Perverseness or Inconsideration of the Prince or People, or both: Nay, when we have pray'd in Aid of Religion, and taken that into our support, what wretched work has Religion it self made in States, and unhinged them, as Learning has Religion? Those very Means that should compose and settle, have subverted, and do still disorder the World. What Mischiefs have not those two words, **Prerogative** and **Liberty**, introduced both in Law and Gospel Construction? and those two Epithets of **Obedience**, **Active** and **Passive**, are sacrific'd to **Forms** more than **Force**; and have been abus'd almost as much by *Government* as *Anarchy*.

In our best Form of Government (as we call it) when the Constitution comes to clash, the sole Question is, Which is to be preferred, the **Person and Will of a Prince**, or the **Law of the Land**? Which is most sacred, the **Power**, or the **Ordonnance**? Which is to be obey'd and maintain'd, the **King** who invades the **Law** and **Religion** Establish'd, (for 'tis certain such a Case hath happen'd) or **Religion** and **Law** which establish'd them? Whether Religion, or the Humour of a King be to be obey'd, even for the sake of Religion?

This

This, it seems, hath been made a Doubt, and hath been a Theme more than sufficiently handled of late Years especially, and managed with Artifice enough (to say no worse) on both sides. Indeed if we were now under a *Theocracy*, the extravagance of the Dispute would be on t'other hand; and if God at this day could be suppos'd to govern our Governors, as in the *Jewish* Oeconomy, when Rulers, Captains, Priests, Judges and Kings, were immediately inspired and led by the Almighty to keep them from stumbling or swerving, before that Kings were given for a Curse, and when not made such; Implicit Faith and Obedience must be then due: But when God himself leaves us to the Rules of Human Laws, as he plainly intimates, and is confest by the most Learned Divines who are impartial, 'tis otherwise: And I must confess, in my poor Opinion (God forgive me if I err, and I err in good Company) under the Gospel God seems not so much concern'd in Human Powers (otherwise than Human Laws): And our Saviour, in his Sermon on the Mount, hath not one word about Kingdoms, (only of another World). After which the Texts of the Apostles are not to be taken in a general extended Sense; for our Saviour himself, who is, and must be suppos'd to comprehend all necessary Instructions for a Christian, (when he insists on superlative Directions) would, no doubt, have vouch-

vouchsafed some Guide in obedience to the Powers on Earth, if he had not concluded them by the Measures of their respective Constitutions; and his Expression of *rendring unto Cesar the things that are Cesar's*, &c. sufficiently implies the force of that Argument; and the Exempt reservation of Property, &c. No doubt the meaning of the Apostles has been strain'd too far by some Divines; and besides, it infers but little to us, forasmuch as they do not, nor ever did agree in their Interpretations; 'twill be to little purpose that the Apostles were inspired if we are not inspired also with an adequate degree of Apprehension. But this only by the by: This is not my Province, and I shall have occasion to resume this Argument hereafter. All that I shall say at present is, That **Arbitrary Power**, and **Legal Right**, are Contradictions, and cannot consist in Human Understandings. Therefore I shall make bold to take *Power* in that sense which may consist with Reason, and Rejecting the first, tack the word *Legal* to it, and shall wave or post-pone the Premisses, from the absurdity of the Conclusion. For if it be allow'd, or may be suppos'd, That a King can with his own breath blow away the Laws of the State, or at second-hand remove the Land-mark; or is to be told by any Metaphysical Pedant, That no Law can bind him, but what proceeds from his own Mouth, nor that neither, any longer than he pleases;

pleases; and by vertue of such a Traiterous Legerdemain, a Prince is to be distinguish'd oft, and absolv'd from a Coronation-Oath, and our Allegiance to be transpos'd or inverted by a barbarous Contradiction of the Term, into a subsequent Obligation: And the Duty of Obedience must shift with the Wind (because the Weathercock was placed upon Churches in pious memory of St. *Peter*, who besides denying Christ, preach'd, as 'tis said, the Doctrine of Passive Obedience also); I'm sure, if this be true, morally speaking, 'twill be nonsense, and to no purpose, to pretend to establish any Laws in Church or State: And our Ancestors had been ev'ry jot as well employ'd at Push-pin (or with *Socrates* and his Boys) playing at Cob-Nut, or riding the Hobby-horse, with as good a grace, as contending for *Magna Charta*: All Government, in short, without the immediate hand of Heaven (which we are not taught by God, or instructed by the Events of Story, to rely on, or expect) will at this rate of Argument become utterly impracticable, and must degenerate into Confusion.

So on the other side, the misapplication of the Constitution of Government may be almost as fatal as the throwing it off. As for instance, in a Mixt or Limited Monarchy, where the Ingredient Qualifications are not duly observ'd, and fairly maintain'd; Sometimes these Forms have prov'd but Snares on the

the Subjects Liberties and Properties: Thus it is when one part of the State encroacheth upon the others; and 'twill be the same thing when they have all together (or two of them) too close and united a Correspondence and Intelligence, and the Trinity in Unity, or *Vice versa* (if I may so speak) are confounded and consolidated: The one part of the Body represented, may thus as well be betray'd out of its Rights, as huffed out of them in the other Case. Where-ever a Constitution is not preserved in its primitive force and dignity, according to the true intent thereof, some part may, and must suffer: A Legislative Power may be as pernicious as an Executive; for 'tis far from impossible, that Injuries may be done under the Colour and Mask of Laws. Sir *William Temple* quotes *Heraclitus* for saying, " The only skill or " knowledge of any value in the Politicks, " was the Secret of governing all by all: And he afterwards remarks, " That what Prince " soever can hit of this Secret, need know " no more for his own Safety and Happiness, " or that of the People he governs: For no " State or Government can be much troubled " or endanger'd by any private Factions, " which is grounded upon the general Con- " sent and Satisfaction of the Subject. Happy Kings, if they would be contented to have kept within the Confines of such Measures! But this is a Doctrine which will not go down with

with Kings: Thus *Germany* flourish'd till *Charles* the V*th*'s time, who introduced higher Reasons of State; till the Jesuits taught the way of bringing the Sovereign Power from the States to the Empire: What hath *Spain* got by the pretence of an Absolute Power, *i. e.* Oppression? It lost *Portugal*, it lost the *Low Countries*, &c. And in truth, the Kings of *Spain* have exerted their Power so far, till they have lost it all; and by Trick of Favourite Ministers, and other Politicks interchangeably transacted and shuffled between them and the *French* Kings, they are now at last scarce in a Condition, by virtue of such Arbitrary Extravagancies, to defend themselves. The Princes of *Italy*, who are so Absolute, only betray their own Weakness by it. And though *France* at present may seem to flourish outwardly, yet who knows not that She groans in her Bowels? Indeed Sir *Robert Cotton* is unhappily mistaken in his Conclusion touching *England*; " That it cannot " groan under a Democracy, which it never " yet felt or fear'd: And the late Times under King *Charles* the First, seem to be an Instance to the contrary, and an Exception to that Rule: But then the Reasons are given by him but just before; *viz.* That such a Government suiting thus with Monarchy, must strictly maintain its Form: And I doubt 'twas something like affecting at Arbitrary Power, exclusive of his Parliament, at least

the

the House of Commons, which brought that Unfortunate Monarch within the Exception to the Rule ; and the Rule may stand good still. Generally speaking, Trick and Fraud seldom make a Second Advantage ; and *Matchiavel*, after all his Noise, instances only in *Alexander* the Sixth, who (he says) thriv'd by it; yet mark the End ; he at last was poyson'd by a Fraud prepared by his Bastard *Borgia* for another. The *French* have a Saying, *L' Addresse surmonte la Force:* But I suppose they are not so harden'd to extend this to all Frauds and Falsifications: There are some Honest Politicks and Stratagems, which a Man of Honour may lawfully use, no doubt, in War, in Peace, in Treaties: Honest, if only that Custom hath given them a sort of Sanction: Though, by the by, of old these Methods were despised by the Braver Heroes, even before Christianity ; which allows us to be *Wise as Serpents*, but *Innocent as Doves*. But all that I contend for in Modern Politicks, is the Exercise of Justice and Honour, which is, or ought to be the Peculiar Character of Kings: And that Sincerity is the likeliest Principle to establish a Nation : And must hold with *Padre Paolo*, That open Honesty and Plain-dealing at last will prevail against Trick and Artifice.

All Laws of Power are, or are supposed to be, founded on the Law of God; and 'tis said, Righteousness supports Crowns : For God's

God's fake, What is the Moral of Prerogative? What is the End of this Abfolute Power? Whence do Kings derive this fuperlative Talent of controuling Mankind? Is it that they have been ftiled and courted as Gods, or their Reprefentatives? Alas! we find they reprefent Man in Underftanding and Failings: 'Tis not therefore that they are infpired with any greater Degree of Perfection or Wifdom: No, we find by Experience they are in this like other Men, fubject to the fame Paffions and Infirmities: As King *James* the Firft faid, They differ not in Stuff: Their Natural Advantages do not afford them fuch Superiority and Pre-eminence in Power, with any Juftice of Human Reafon. This great Deference and Submiffion which they claim as due to their Character, muft be either, That God once vouchfafed them his Supernatural Affiftance; or, That now Kings are prefumed to have the Affiftance of a Better and Wifer Council. If the firft, the Signs are vanifhed; if the latter, 'tis confefs'd due, fubject to the Rules and Forms of the General Law of Nations, and the Municipal Laws of the Land; on fuppofition that Kings act and labour by the joint Concurrence of Wife and Legal Councels for the Publick Good of the Commonwealth. Hence it is that they are endow'd with greater Privilege; Hence it is that they are intitled to (what is call'd) Prerogative, to

pafs

pass over the Definitions given by *Bracton* and *Britton*, and *Fortescue*'s foolish Etimology. There must be a Prerogative somewhere in all Places. There is a Prerogative in Kings by the Law of Nations; and the Use of it is to shew Mercy, to reward Virtue: 'Tis the Law that punisheth, not Kings; and because there is no written Equity in Criminal or Capital Matters, therefore the Seat of Mercy is placed by the Fountain of Justice. This is, no doubt, properly and truly to be God's Vicegerent. Thus with us, *Potest Rex ei, lege suâ Dignitatis Condonare, si velit, Mortem promeritam:* Spoken of *Edward* the Confessor. Though there is a sort of Equity by the Letter of our Law in the Case of Manslaughter, making an allowance for the Passions of Men; and the King's Pardon of Murder hath been question'd; it looks like a Dispensing with the Positive Law of God: It is certain he can't change the Punishment. There are several Prerogatives and Flowers of the Crown, some of Use, some for Ornament, but founded also upon Reason. The King hath all Mines of Gold and Silver, *Treasure Trove,* Escheats of all Cities: May take his Creditors into Protection, till he be satisfied with Preference: May take Body, Lands, and Goods of Debtor, &c. because the King's Treasure is supposed to be for the publick Benefit. May make any Foreign Coin lawful

Spelman Gloss. Prærogativa Regis.

Money

Money of *England* by Proclamation; for Exigencies may require it. The King may dig in the Subjects House (not Mansion-House or Barn) for Salt petre, being for the Defence of the Nation. Kings only can have Parks and Chaces, and not Subjects, without his License: So Swans in Royal Rivers, because they are stately Creatures, and Royal Game, and become the Honour of a King. The King shall be said to be Founder, though another join in the Foundation, &c. because 'tis for his Honour. The King shall have Ward, though the Lands were held of him by Posteriority, because the King's Title shall be preferr'd, and not put in Competition with the Subject. So he shall not be Tenant in common; *i. e.* He shall have all, because a Subject ought not to be equal with him in any thing. There are also several other Franchises which by the Policy of our Law belong to the Crown: And we say in our Law, That the King's Prerogative is part of the Law of *England*, and comprehended within the same. We say also, That the King hath no Prerogative but that which the Law of the Land allows him: And 'tis certain he is restrained in several respects by our Law, as in a Politick Capacity: Letting pass those Distinctions and Cant in *Coke*'s 7th *Rep. Calvin*'s Case of the King's Prerogative. As he hath Advantages, so he hath his Disadvantages also; at least, Kings, or or others for them, are apt to call them so. Thus he can't by Testament dispose of the Jewels of the Crown; 'tis doubted whether he may legally pawn them, though it be said he may give them by his Letters-Patents; 'tis against the Honour of the Crown: The Law is so jealous of the King's Honour, that it hath preferr'd it before his Profit. He hath no Prerogative against *Magna Charta*; cannot take or prejudice the Inheritance of any: Can't send any man out of the Realm against his Will, because he hath the Command of the Service of the Subjects only for Defence of the Realm: Can't lay any new Impost on Merchandises. Can take none but usual and Ancient Aids and Taxes. Can't dispense with Statutes made for Publick Good, or against *Nusances*, or *Mala in se*; Can do no Wrong; Can't alter the Law, Common or Ecclesiastical; Nor Statute-Law, or Custom of the Realm, by Proclamation or otherwise: Nor create any Offence thereby, which was not an Offence before. Can't grant a Corporation any new Jurisdiction to proceed by Civil Law, because it may deprive Subjects hereby of Privilege of Trial. The King can't put off the Offices of Justice of a King; is not suppos'd to be ill-affected, but deceiv'd, and impos'd upon, and abus'd: *Eadem presumitur mens Regis, quæ est juris*, &c.

But

But the late Sticklers for Arbitrary Power have found out a Plea for the Absoluteness of Kings, which as they think, carries some Face of an Objection against the fettering their Prerogative: Say they, At this rate a King can never exert himself as he ought, to do any Glorious Action; or as King *James* the II^d phras'd it, to *Carry the Reputation of a Kingdom high in the World*: He cannot extend his Conquests, *&c.* No matter whether he can or not: Neither can he oppress his Subjects: It is sufficient for Kings (especially for a King of *Great Britain*) to be on the Defensive by Land, neither do I believe any of our Kings ever got any thing by extending their Dominions. 'Tis no Argument to us in our Situation, if the matter were so: But this Notion is a Mistake: For never did any King do extraordinary Feats, where he made War, and carried it on against the Inclinations, or without the Consent of his People: The Fights with the *Dutch* at Sea, in the Reign of King *Charles* the II^d, is a sufficient Instance of this Nature: We fought against the Grain, and without an Enemy, as Sir *William Temple* observes. Nor shall we find in History, that any King hath continued his enlarged Bounds, where he carried on Imposts and Taxes by Violence at Home, to the Impoverishing of his People. Let the End of this present *French* King be observ'd, who seems to stand an Exception

on at present, but he stands a very ticklish one. Besides, the true Interest and Advantage of our Island lies another way : To maintain the Sovereignty of the Seas; to promote Trade and Traffick, &c. And to this purpose the King hath the highest Prerogative in this Element: He may press Men for this Service, which he cannot for any Foreign Expedition by Land: He hath Customs, Tunnage and Poundage, &c. Yet not these without Consent in Parliament; and some of our Kings have made but a scurvy Experiment, in attempting to take them without it. Whence then doth come this Title to Arbitrary Absolute Power? It must be the Child of Conquest, or some other Paramount Inherent Right. And to this purpose it is objected, That by our Laws we acknowledge several Rights and Privileges of the Subject to be Concessions from Kings; and we yield the Lands to be holden immediately or mediately of the Crown, &c. This is pretended to found in Conquest rather than Compact, or to be founded on the Patriarchal Right: And Sir *Robert Filmer* especially is pleasant upon Sir *Edward Coke* for this: He says, " If the first Kings were " chosen by the People (as many think they " were), then surely our Forefathers were a " very bountiful (if not prodigal) People, " to give all the Lands of the whole King- " dom to their Kings, with liberty to them
" to

"to keep what they pleas'd, and to give the
"Remainder to their Subjects, clogg'd and
"incumbred with a Condition to defend the
"Realm: This is but an ill sign of a Limited
"Monarchy by Original Constitution or
"Contract. At this rate a Man who writes with the Fancy of a Government, may expose any thing, even himself. But why doth this necessarily follow? May not several Privileges and Powers be lodged in the Crown, for Conformity and Dignity of Government, by Consent? And so, May not Estates, or the Lands of a Kingdom, be divided by Contract, with the acknowledgment of the Tenure, and to express the Service? How come Lands to Escheat to the Crown, (for they are forfeited for Treason) I mean of Cities, but that there is no Heir? How comes the King to have the Year, Day, and Waste of Lands, which Escheat to the Lord? By what Law, if not of Contract? To say they moved from the King, and were Limitations of his Bounty, is as much suppos'd on the other hand, and *gratis dictum.* If he had virtually all Lands, Why not all Goods, &c. too? No man will say that. If he had, I confess there would be then no use of Parliaments. But to proceed, the King by his Prerogative may Call, and Prorogue, and Dissolve Parliaments: By what Law had he this Prerogative? If not by Law of Compact and Consent, of Necessity to avoid
Con-

Confusion; for if he could Command his Subjects Purses, &c. there could not otherwise be any Original use of them: He might, and would, no doubt, have call'd and made use of only a Privy, or Cabinet Council, or Cabal; for after this way of Inference, no King would certainly have Clogg'd himself with the impertinent Formalities of a Parliament; their Predecessors were very Weak, or Prodigal to Clip their own Wings, and give their Subjects a share in the Legislative Power: This is but an ill sign of an Original, Absolute, Arbitrary Power: And 'twas upon this pretence, though those Gentlemen don't care to own it, That they would have endeavoured to Disengage their King from the use of Parliaments, and would conclude, That the King might chuse, whether he would ever call any or not, at least in this Form. Thus they would beg the Question, and presume the Consequence on their side; because equally absurd. The King may Proclaim War, &c. Does it follow therefore that he may make it without other Heads and Hands? Thus they confound the Executive and Legislative Authority. They say Scribling is a sign of a Licentious Age, and some think of a Decaying State too: Ought not some Creaturs to be Muzled? There were many odd sort of extravagant Books published on Subjects of this Nature, in the Reign of King *Charles* the II[d]; not without

Reason,

Reason, as we may suppose: But all these violent pursuits in both Extremes, are suspitious; and where all Parties mean nothing but the Publick Good, there's nothing of this nature worth contending for. And whoever will reflect on the Circumstances, and Occasions, or Times of such Publications, and the advancing these high-flown Notions, with a little pains of Comparison, will easily see through the Mystery of their Policy.

It is very extraordinary, That Subjects make Kings Conquerors in spight of their Teeths, and against their own Professions and Declarations, on purpose to make themselves Slaves by their own Consequence; though this really is neither the true Signification nor Import, as Mr *Spelman* makes appear in his Glossary; let them take it in their own sense; but we may assure our selves they did not intend to inslave themselves. They tell us, That *William* the Ist was a Conqueror, and therefore we were all Slaves, &c. (though at other times Force and Success will make no Right): Yet afterwards they also tell us, when we come to insist on our Rights as Subjects, That *Magna Charta* was obtained by Force, &c. What then? So had the Crown been before (it seems) by them: Either the People of *England* had some Legal Rights before the Conquest, or not: If they had (as is confess'd), 'twas time to endeavour the Restoring of them. If *William*

liam the Ist were an Intruder, and came in by Force of Arms only, he was but a Succeſsful Uſurper; and the People being under a Force, could not loſe their Rights: If he came in with pretence of Title, Title continued them in their Rights; and either way was juſtifiable. I am engaged in this matter before I am aware, and beyond my firſt intention, and I ſhall meet with theſe Gentlemen anon. But not to foreſtal you in the Hiſtory, I can't avoid a Hint upon thoſe times, being upon *Magna Charta*, and that being by that Act declared to be Declaratory of the Fundamental Rights and Common Laws of the Realm: To ſhew the Arts of Debauching Kings, and the end of ſuch Attempts, in one previous Inſtance;
" *Hubert de Burgo* (as you may ſee in Sir *Ed-*
" *ward Coke*'s *Preface* to *Magna Charta, &c.*)
" meaning to make his ſtep to Ambition,
" (which ever Rideth without Reins) per-
" ſuaded and humoured that King, That he
" might avoid that Charter of his Father
" King *John*, by *Dureſs*, and his own great
" Charter, and *Charta de Foreſta* alſo, for that
" he was within Age; whereupon the King
" got one of the great Charters, and that of
" the Foreſt into his Hands, and by his Coun-
" cel unjuſtly *Cancell'd* both the ſaid Charters;
" though this *Hubert de Burgo* was *Primier*
" Witneſs of all the Temporal Lords to both
" the ſaid Charters; whereupon he became
" in

"in high Favour with the King, &c. But soon after (for Flattery, and Flatterers have no sure Foundation) he fell into the King's heavy Indignation; and after many fearful and miserable Troubles, he was Justly, and according to Law, Sentenc'd by his Peers in open Parliament, and as justly Degraded of the Dignity which he had unjustly obtained, &c.

So that other Notion of Paternal Right is as Extraordinary: This takes a short way, and makes Mankind Rebels from the Creation, or from the Flood. Who could have imagined, That this Paternal Dominion from *Adam* could have been inferr'd from that Expression of the *Psalmist*, *The earth hath he given to the children of men?* Which Sir Robert Filmer (learnedly) says, *Doth shew that the Title of Government comes from Fatherhood.* Methinks it seems a more plausible and literal Argument to Exclude Fathers, (or to lay them aside, as they do in some Countries, at such an Age): Why have not this Party a scruple of Conscience about all other Variations of Government, even by God himself? At this rate they ought to procure Masses for the Souls of their Progenitors who lived in the Heptarchy: It is certain, no body living under any Commonwealth can hope to be Saved, as remaining in a continued state of Rebellion. Thus they create a double Obligation on Men, and

harrass

harrass their very Souls between their Natural and Political Parents, in virtue of the Fifth Commandment: But as much a *Frenchman* as he seems to be, I know not how he will excuse *Pharamond* for introducing the *Salique Law*, nor the Nobless of the Country for encouraging it; for the Commandment says, *Honour thy Mother* also. I hope Sir *Robert Filmer* had no Gavelkind Land; the Custom of Tanestry and Borough-*English*, must also be abominable in his sight; which to other Men seem to be built upon good natural Principles of Reason. But (seriously) what indifferent Person (if there can be any such in the World) will, without indignation, digest such sort of Debates? After the same fashion Sir *Robert Filmer* gives us farther to understand; "He cannot learn, "That either the *Hebrew*, *Greek*, or *Latin*, "have any proper Original Word for a "*Tyrant* or *Slave*; it seems these are of "late invention, and taken up in Disgrace "of Monarchical Government." Why not more Charitably, as well as more truly, from the Experience of the Abuses in the Exercise of such Monarchical, or Absolute Powers? And he himself had given the reason but just before, *viz.* "That the *Greek* and "*Latin* Authors liv'd in Popular Governments: For which reason, no doubt, there was no occasion for such Monstrous and Barbarous Terms. But he could not be in earnest

nest in this Observation; I must appeal from his Sincerity, to his Judgment. He does well to bar all other Schemes but his own: "He forbids us to rely on *Aristotle*, the "Grand Master of Politicks; or the *Greek* "or *Latin* Historians, who liv'd in Popular "Times: Though Monsieur *Rapin* allows *Aristotle*, &c. to be us'd in Divinity, and says, St. *Thomas*, and other Divines, have us'd him with good success.

But others, and they Divines and Bishops too, have lately told us, That we are not to rely on Scripture in such Cases. In what a condition is poor Subject Man? And what was all this to the purpose? when Scripture it self doth not peremptorily conclude us, but leaves us at large to the Laws and Usages of Countries, to the Ordinances of Man, as Sir *Robert* himself confesses, though with a lamentable strain upon St. *Paul* and St. *Peter*. Every one saw what was aim'd at, and offer'd by way of deduction from those Topicks of Doctrinal Government: But because Sir *Robert* sends us to *France* to School to be inform'd in our Constitution, and very much affects *French* Policy (for he wrote in a time when the *French* Air was predominant); let us see whether the Kings of *France* themselves did always talk in this Language: Whether they have been continually so uniform in this Fancy of Absolute Power, for the disposing of themselves, and their

their Kingdoms: *Francis* the First (who was Contemporary with our *Henry* the Eighth, and as Haughty a Prince, and was attended with the Flattery of Courtiers too) when he was taken Prisoner at the Battel of *Pavia*, afterwards for Answer to the Proposals sent him by the Emperor for his Release, amongst other things, says, " That they were not in
" his power, because they shock'd the Funda-
" mental Laws of *France*, to which he was
" subjected, *&c.* After he was at liberty,
" having call'd an Assembly of the most No-
" table Persons of the Three Estates of the
" Kingdom for their Advice touching the
" delivery of his Children and himself, prof-
" fering to return to Prison, if they thought
" fit; Their *Orders* all answer'd separately,
" That his Person was the Kingdom's, not
" his; and as touching the restoring of *Bur-*
" *gundy*, That it was a Member of the
" Crown, whereof he was but Usufructua-
" ry; That therefore he could not dispose of
" the one or t'other. But withal they offer'd
" him Two Millions of Gold for the Ransom
" of his Children, and assur'd him, That if
" it must come to a War, they would nei-
" ther spare their Lives nor Fortunes. I'm
sorry no Precedent will serve for our Imitation, but only that of the present *French* King, and his Ally the *Great Turk*: In the sense of these Authors, theirs must be the only Apostolick Orthodox Institution. We

Mez. Chron 5

are

are told also, That there is a Place, where, whenever the King spits, the greatest Ladies of his Court put out their Hands to receive it: And another Nation, where the most Eminent Persons about him stoop to take up his Ordure in a Linnen Cloth: And other People, where no Subject speaks to the King, but through a Trunk; and there are, no doubt, several other such like Fantastick Customs of Submission, and Idolatrous Reverence: What then? Every Land is still nevertheless to be guided by its own Customs and Laws: And I wish some of these Absolute Arbitrary-Power-Sparks liv'd in one of the last mention'd Places. In earnest, Flattery is a most sordid and pernicious Vice, and we were lately very near drawing down Judgments on our selves for it; and had like to have suffer'd for pretending to offer Sacrifices which were never meant. This Stuff of Passive Submission to Arbitrary Tyrannical Powers, could never be offer'd to sale in a true Light: The Doctrine would stink in the Nostrils of a Good King, who had any thing of Virtue, Piety, or good Nature: A King, who, to use the words of King *James* the First, "Acknowledges himself *ordain'd* "*for his People*, having received from God "a Burthen of Government, whereof he "must be Accountable; and a good King "thinketh his highest Honour to consist in "the due Discharge of his Calling; and em-
"ployeth

"ployeth all his study and pains to procure; "and maintain, by the making and executing "of Good Laws, the Welfare and Peace of "his People; and as the Natural Father and "kindly Master thinketh his greatest Con- "tentment standeth in their Prosperity, and "his greatest Surety in having their Hearts. This, as to the Political and Moral part of Government. And as to the matter of Religion: What is it but to inspire a King with Persecution? What must this come to, when Kings have different Educations, and different Tutors to catechize them, if the Civil Establishment be not our Standard, and the Law our Protection in Church as well as State? As to the Case where the King and the Laws are of the same persuasion, If Recusants and Dissenters are so unfortunate as to fall under a Prosecution for their particular Opinions, be it at the peril of the King's Conscience, and those who advise him; but here, and here only is the true Notion of being Passive; and I must confess I can't tell how to help them: Here I think they must suffer, and not resist, but fly to another City, if they do not like that where the Government legally sits upon their Skirts. Though I know some don't allow the Legislative Power to intermeddle with Religion, as having too much a Lay mixture for the Pallet of the Church; Yet, for my part, I do not see how otherwise we could maintain any

Esta-

Establishment in it: For though since the Reformation, the King, as Head, hath the Supremacy devolv'd on him, and 'tis consented that he may make Canons to bind the Clergy even without a Convocation; yet as the Church does not allow him to speak with his own Mouth, or Act with his own Hands in the Administration of Essentials of Religion, so the State doth not in the Alterations of them: So that he is not Absolute or Independent either in his Ecclesiastical or Civil Capacity of Policy: And therefore the whole Constitution, and Three Estates, must necessarily be call'd in on all Occasions of Change in Discipline, or Innovation of Rites, as well as in the alteration and repealing of other Old Laws, or introducing and declaring New ones. This by way of Parenthesis; But I was speaking of Sir *Robert Filmer*'s Patriarchal Power, and the Extravagancies he infers from thence, grounded, as he pretends, from Scripture. Therefore I would only ask him one Question more: Was there no such proper Word in the *Hebrew*, *Greek*, or *Latin*, for Tyrant, or Slave? Pray how then came the Words and Doctrine of *Non-Resistance* and *Passive Obedience* into the *Greek*? It must be only taken up of late by some such Authors, in disgrace of Monarchical Government, according to Law; and to put Obedience, as Legal, out of countenance; To bring People to submit blindly to *Arbitrary Power*.

There

There is the word Τύραννῷ in *Greek*, which signifies at least, *King* or *Prince*: But is there any one doubts, that there has been such a thing as a Harsh, Unreasonable, and Unnatural Father or King? It must follow then, that the Obedience intended by the Apostles (who wrote in *Greek*) was only to the Laws, and the Legal Exercise of them, according to the Usage of their respective Places, which made them Legal: Or to Kings, as not being a terror to the Good, but only to the Evil: But it would tire even Patience it self to follow these sort of Gentlemen in all their Confused By-ways. Therefore to return more immediately to my Subject, and to my Friend *Seigneur de Montaigne*, whom I am not asham'd to own, let the Grave and Wise say what they will; for I must ever have a greater Respect for an Author who talks judiciously of Trifling Matters (if they be so), than for One who talks triflingly on Judicious Subjects. He tells us, "These Great "and Tedious Debates about the best Form "of Society, and the most Commodious "Rules to bind us, are Debates only proper "for the Exercise of our Wits; and all the "Descriptions of Policies, feign'd by Art, are "found to be ridiculous, and unfit to be "put in practice. And in another place, "Not according to Opinion, but in Truth "and Reality, The best and most Excellent "Government for every Nation, is that un-
"der

"der which it is maintain'd: This *Montaigne* says, who express'd and practis'd as great Loyalty as ever any Man of Sense and Honour did; and I agree with him, "That all "Reverence and Submission is due to Kings, "except that of the Understanding. This as a Gentleman; and as a Christian, he farther adds, "Christian Religion hath all the "Marks of utmost Utility and Justice, but "none more manifest than the severe Injun-"ction it lays indifferently upon all, to "yield absolute Obedience to the Civil Ma-"gistracy, and to maintain and defend the "Laws: *i.e.* in *English*, To submit according to Law. And all Policy, as well as Religion, enforces Obedience to the Administrators of Right and Justice: And if it be permitted to argue from Etymologies (which is surer than from Examples) the *Grecians* tell us the word πόλις signifies *Ubi homines versantur, vel potius a πολύς quod sint πολλοὶ certis legibus juncti*: And we may assure our selves, That People would not build Houses, *&c.* till the Possession and Enjoyment of them was establish'd by certain Laws. But we shall never have done, never come to any settlement, if the Forms of Government and Laws are not admitted, but suffer'd to be disputed at this time of day. We are therefore to take Laws as we find them, and as they stand in use and practice by a continued Establishment: It can't be material therefore to look

back

back how the Figure of our Legiflative Power ftood a Thoufand Years ago, or from a much fhorter date of Time; How the Form of Writs, iffued to the Commons, was heretofore: (though, no doubt, the beft Authority is with them, and it is confeft they were always a Conftituent part of the Legiflative Power); as 'tis idle and impertinent to fay, The Supreme or Legiflative Power muft be ever Arbitrary; this is an abfurd Affirmation, when all Parties in a Nation agree by their Reprefentatives to the Enaction of Laws. By the Laws of God and Man, Our Conftitution ought now to reft in Peace in an Inviolable Eftablifhment: Kings fwear, as our *Saviour* preach'd in the Mount, to the Multitude: A King's Coronation-Oath muft be interpreted, *ad Captum Populi*, and to ordinary Intendment; That fo there may be fome certain Rule of Governing, and true Meafures of Obeying, whereby the whole Community may be preferv'd in Peace and Order, which is the End of all Government.

We in *England* feem to value our felves more peculiarly on the Polity of our Conftitution: There hath been enough faid in praife of our Laws: No doubt they are very good, if well obferv'd; fo good at leaft, 'That I never heard that any King of *England* ever pretended to except againft them, when he was ask't the Queftion at his Coronation,

nation, Whether he would Obfe[rve the]
Laws? and fo Good, That the Sub[ject, as]
far as I perceive) defires only the C[onfirma]-
tion and Continuance of them. An[d I may]
be bold to fay, for the Honour of the [English]
Nation and People, (notwithftandin[g what]
Name fome are pleas'd to give us a[t home]
and abroad at prefent) That there w[as not]
any War in *England*, from the *Barons* [Wars to]
the late *Civil War*, (fetting afide the [Wars]
between the H. of Y. and L.) bu[t what]
was occafion'd and begun on Colou[r of the]
King's impofing an Arbitrary Pow[er on]
the Rights and Privileges of the [People,]
and after Complaint and Applicat[ion for]
Redrefs of Grievances, and Reftit[ution of]
their Rights and Privileges; and a[ll other]
Nations have done the fame whe[n they]
could; (I fpeak of the beginning o[f Wars,]
I do not always juftify the End of [them.)]
And muft aver, That the People of [England]
in general, have, notwithftanding t[he Pro]-
verb, which is Exotick, been alway[s good]
natur'd Subjects: Eafy enough to be [impos'd]
upon, and cajoled out of their Mon[ey, and]
their Lives, for the Service of the C[rown.]
And, as I think, fo Modeft, that th[ey have]
never affum'd, as Men, to ftand in c[ompeti]-
tion with Majefty, nor have ever pre[tended]
to be fo much as Kings, till Kings we[re per]-
fuaded to think themfelves more than [Men.]
Hence, as you will perceive, in the [...]

Government of England.

following Remarks, have (for the most part) sprung those Jealousies which divided King and People, and disjointed the United Common Interest of Both. Ambitious and Designing Men have rais'd Phantoms of Powers and Laws, which had being only in the Clouds, at least had none amongst us: And Imaginary Constructions have been put upon those, which were plain and obvious. The Terms of *Power* and *Subjection* have been so artificially debated, and the Laws of God and Nature, the Law of Reason, and that of Nations, so partially and sillily, as well as learnedly confounded, that the true Idea of our own Govenment and Law was perplex'd and lost. So that no wonder if Mistaken Principles sometimes misled King and People, where they might mean well enough both; and at other times either King or People might have a latitude of construing them perversely, when they did not so.

Now though 'tis confess'd we cannot arrive at any degree of Perfection in Government (nor any thing else) here in this troublesome uncertain World; Yet Experience convinceth us, That some Times have been better than others; and that this Nation hath been happier under some Princes than Others, i.e. happier under those whose Conduct and Government have agreed best with the Laws and Constitutions. The only Design of these passing-Observations and Reflections, is

to

to point out the Errors, and set a Mark on the Rocks, that we may avoid them: To shew Kings and People the Principles and Practises by which they Miscarried or Succeeded, upon Rational Grounds, and Natural Consequences; so that Measures may be taken which may more probably secure the Peace and Welfare of this Nation for the future. I go no farther back than the Conquest or Descent here by King *William* the First; That being (as I think) enough for our Instruction; enough to Inform, without confounding our Memories and Judgments.

WILLIAM

WILLIAM I.

NOT to play the *Grammarian* on Words, nor to repeat Old Stories; though I can scarce pass by Mr. *Spelman*'s Definition of him; *Conquestor dicitur qui Angliam conquisivit, i. e. acquisivit*, purchas'd, *non quod subegit*. But to take *William the Conqueror* (as they call him) in the usual Acceptation, there can be but little Observable during the Transactions of his Reign, to ground Remarks of Civil Policy. As he trimmed between Conquest and Title (by Gift from *Ed. the Confessor*, he was also Kin by his Mother's side) so he divided his Government between Acts of Justice and Wrong; not to mention the old Story of *Warren* the *Norman*, and *Sharnborn* an *Englishman*: It is plain the *Kentishmen* had their Laws Confirm'd to them by Treaty, and were never Conquered. He granted to the City of *London* their Charters as they had them in the Time of Saint *Edward*: 'Tis true, he Alter'd the Laws, and introduced the *French* Language; but the Alteration seems to be for the

the better, and he was generally Juſt to the Laws which were made: He alter'd Paſtimes alſo, and 'twas of courſe, for *Engliſhmen* are ever fond of New things. The worſt thing he did, was Depopulating ſo many Towns, and overthrowing ſo many Churches, for Thirty Miles round, to make a Chaſe, or New Foreſt in *Hampſhire*; and the Execution of ſevere Laws againſt Deſtroyers of Deer, or Game, by putting out their Eyes, *&c.* for which, for ought I know, his Two Sons and Nephew might come to untimely Ends in the ſame place. But in the main, he was modeſt enough for a Prince who came in with his Sword in his Hand: And at laſt, after all his Buſtle, he was forced, as it were, to come to a Parly with the *Engliſh* Nobility, and before they laid down their Arms, this mighty Conqueror engaged for Peace, and after, in the preſence of Archbiſhop *Lanfrank* and others, took a Solemn Oath upon the Evangeliſts, and all the Relicks of the Church of St. *Albans*, from thenceforth to Obſerve and Keep the Good and Ancient Laws of the Realm, which the Noble Kings of *England*, his Predeceſſors, had before Made and Ordained, but eſpecially thoſe of Saint *Edward*; which, as is ſaid, were ſuppos'd of all others to be the moſt Equal and Indifferent for the general Good of the People. If the Churchmen can Forgive him (for he Repented of it) the taking

them

them down somewhat in their Temporal Power, and calling in the *Jews*; they may forget his Ransacking the Monasteries, if thep please, also, because he spared the Profits of Vacant Abbies and Bishopricks. His Life ended in a Circle; and as he pretended to take the Crown by Gift, so he disposed of it, and left it by Gift also.

WILLIAM

WILLIAM II.

DURING this King's Time, the Government and Laws seem to be in a continued Ferment and State of War. As he was attack'd on all Hands, and put to great Charges, so he spared neither Church nor State for Taxations, but pillaged both in an unreasonable extravagant manner. It is said he doubted of some Points of Religion; but one would rather believe he doubted of it all, by his Life, and Expression to the *Jews*, and the Management of Churchmen and their Benefices, and Religious Houses: He Died so suddenly, that he had not time to tell his Opinion at his Death. If he did not keep his Word so devoutly as he ought; if he was trifling in things appertaining to Religion, and profanely free with the Patrimony of the Church, the Historians of that Age have assign'd him the Judgments of God in the End; and I shall leave him to the *Pope*'s Mercy, for with-holding *Peter Pence*. In this King's Reign we find the first Exercise of a Prerogative; which seems reasonable and natural enough, in forbidding his Subjects by Proclamation to go out of the

Land

Land without Licenſe, if it had been grounded on a good Deſign; but being introduced only, firſt to make his Subjects uneaſy at Home, and after to get Money out of them for a Licenſe to go Abroad; the Occaſion diſgraceth the Thing, which otherwiſe had been juſtifiable on a true foundation, *viz.* To require the Service of the Subject at Home; for the Command of the Aid of the Perſons of his People, is as much an inherent Right in the Crown, as any can be in his own Dominions, though not ſo to Command them out of them on his Service Abroad. He alſo kept his Money from going to *Rome*; and, I ſuppoſe, we ought not to be Angry with any King for keeping his Men and his Money at Home.

HENRY I.

THEY who Write this King's Life, do so vary in his Character, that it is somewhat difficult to Adjust it: But we always ought to speak the best of Kings, if the matter will any ways bear it. Whether he came to the Crown with a just Title or not, he came with a just degree of Understanding and Inclinations to do Justice: He was Born of a King in *England*, and Queen of Royal *English* Blood, as Sir *John Hayward* says; though I know not how he makes it out well; and is said therefore to have raised the Depressed *English* Nation again unto Honour and Credit, and took off their Badges of Slavery, and seems truly Endowed with Kingly Principles; though *Cambden* will have it, That he was Just even to a Fault; Pray God That were the only Fault of Kings. Whatever hath been said to his Disadvantage, he appears, for the most part, to have Governed by the Laws of the Land: And as he gave a Measure to others, he himself made the Laws a Measure of his Prerogative. It will not be worth Enquiry,

quiry, Whether he first Instituted a Parliament in the Form it now stands: He raised Money in a Parliamentary way; we find in his First Parliament at *Salisbury*, he obtained Three Shillings upon every Hide of Land, towards the Marriage of his Daughter with the Emperor, although 'tis said there, these Aids were due by Common Law from the King's Tenants by Knight's Service, *viz.* Aid to Ransom the King's Person; Aid to make the King's Eldest Son a Knight, and Aid to Marry the King's Eldest Daughter once. And although this matter was ascertain'd afterwards by King *John*'s Charter at *Running-Mead*, yet following Kings have not been so tender and reserv'd in this Point. If he may be said to be Cruel to his Brother *Robert*, I'm sure he was very Honourable towards *Lewis* of *France*, when in *England*, whither he came on his own Head, notwithstanding he was Solicited and Tempted to make him away. As to his Personal Virtues or Vices, they were to himself: If he fail'd in the Oeconomicks, he had Troubles in his own House; and whether his Misfortunes of this kind were occasioned by Judgments, or the Follies of himself, or Wife, it is certain he had his share of them; but he took so much care that the Nation knew but very few troubles during his Reign. And as he obtained a Kingdom by a sort of Artifice, so he used his Prerogative with Discretion.

STEPHEN.

STEPHEN.

THIS King's Reign was almost one entire Scene of Military Actions, without any mixture of Civil Policy; he did not live a Year to Enjoy or Manage Peace after his Agreement with *Henry* II. the Son of *Maud:* And there was never any formal Meeting of the Body of the Estates in his time: The Expences of his War were occasioned by a troubled Title, and he maintained them by Confiscations; and although he had continued Charges that way, yet he required few or no Tributes from the People. 'Tis said he had another way of getting Money, *viz.* by causing Men to be Impleaded and Fined for Hunting in his Forests, after he had given them Liberty to Hunt there. For thus far, at least, the Kings Exercised an Absolute Prerogative (only) over the Beasts of the Forest: Which is a Prerogative, I confess, they ought to Enjoy Indisputably.

HENRY II.

THOUGH this King came to the Crown by the moſt Abſolute Title and Cleareſt Right, yet in Four and thirty Years time, we do not find that he pretended to impoſe upon his People any Arbitrary Power; but by Succeſs and Policy he added to the Crown of *England*, *Scotland*, *Ireland*, the Iſles of *Orcades*, *Britain*, *Poytiers*, *Guyen*, and other Provinces of *France*: And for all this he had only one Tax of Eſcuage towards his War with *France*. His cauſing the Caſtles to be Demoliſhed, was a juſtifiable piece of Policy, for the reaſon given, as being Nurſeries of Rebellion. In the beginning of his Reign he refined and reformed the Laws, and 'tis ſaid, made them more Tolerable, and Profitable to his People than they were before; and, what is better, Governed himſelf by them. We do not find the Puniſhments of Capital Offences, or others, were certain, but variable and diſtinguiſhed in the ſame Crime, according to the degrees of Aggravation. The Church-Chroniclers beſtow a Judgment upon him for refuſing to take the Protection of the Diſtreſſed Chriſtians in *Jerusalem*, offered to him by *Heraclius* the Patriarch, and assign his Troubles at Home to that Cause; but they might be mistaken, and he might (as he apprehended) have had greater from his own Sons, if he had gone Abroad upon that Errand. And if the Church will forgive him the Story of *Thomas Becket*, (for he was otherwise very Civil to it) the State had no reason to complain of him; for he suffered neither his Wars nor his Pleasures to be Chargeable to the Nation, nor his Concubines to be Spungers on the People.

RICHARD

RICHARD I.

THERE is but little Observable in the Reign of this King with relation to the Subject at Home, he being the greater part of it out of the Land. If his Artifices of Raising Money were not Justifiable, the occasion may at least Excuse him: He obtained a Subsidy towards his necessary Charges of War; what was properly called Taxation, was by Parliament, or by the Subjects own Contribution and Method of Charging themselves with, as the Money raised for his Ransom. If he may be charged with some slips in Justice, he made it up in Courtesy (which, by the by, goes a great way with *Englishmen*, for 'tis observed, they may be Led, tho' they will not well Drive). And upon his return Home from the Holy Land, we find the first thing he did, was to give his Lords and People Thanks for their Faithfulness to him in his Absence, and for their readiness to Supply him for his Ransom.

JOHN.

Montaigne says in one of his Essays (and he speaks it upon Observation of History): "That Women, Children and Madmen, have had the Fortune to govern Great Kingdoms equally well with the Wisest Princes: And *Thucydides*, That the Stupid more frequently do it, than those of better Understanding. Whether this be an Argument of a Providential Disposing and Governing of Kingdoms, I leave to those that are conversant that way. Some Men, perhaps, may be apt to think it reflects Disgrace on Dignities, if this be true. Some Kings are involv'd in such a Cloud of Circumstances of Difficulty and Intrigues, that there is no looking into them, nor making any Judgment of their Actions. *Speed* guesses of King *John*, "That if his Reign had not fallen out in the time of so Turbulent a Pope, such Ambitious Neighbour Princes, and such Disloyal Subjects; nor his Story into the Hands of Exasperated Writers, he had appear'd a King of as great Renown as Misfortunes: This is civilly and gently said.

This is certain, This King (as all others, when once they have broke through their Coronation-Oath) presently became, as it were, infatuated and deaf to all good Counsel, stoop't to every thing that was mean and base; and having once laid aside his Native Honour, run into all Dishonourable Sordid Actions: The History represents him pursuing his Profit, and even his Pleasures by all manner of Injustice: He prosecuted his Brother, *Geoffry* Archbishop of *York*, and took from him all he had, only for doing the Duty of a Wise and Faithful Councellor. Hence his Lords grew Resty, and refused to follow him into *France*, unless he would restore to them their Rights and Liberties which he had invaded: And when he shuffled with them in the Grant of their Demands, What Wars, what Miseries did not follow? Wars at Home, Foreiners call'd in, the Nation plunder'd and spoil'd, Money procured by Base poor-spirited Tricks; He on one Side forc'd to truckle to the Pope, and (as is said) to submit to somebody worse; his Subjects on the other hand calling in to their Relief (as they thought) a Foreiner, fetch't in *Lewis*, the Son of *Philip* the *French* King; the People in general not living like Men, nor dying like Christians, nor having Christian Burial; the whole Nation one dismal Scene of Horrid

rid Misfortunes: Behold the Effect of Violated Faith and Arbitrary Oppression! But it is no great Credit to Prerogative, That this King, who had no very good Title, unless it were Election, was the first Vindicator of it, in a violent manner: And asserted the Right to Absolute Power with the same Justice, as he did That to the Crown in the time of *Arthur* his Nephew, who was the Undoubted Heir. By these means he brought himself and People into Troubles, which never ended but with his Life.

HENRY III.

HERE we may perceive, as also in another Reign or two hereafter, how the Irregularities of a Father or Predecessor involve the Son and Successor in a Remainder of Troubles, and the Nation also in their intail'd Misfortunes: " For al-
" though those Lords (as Sir *Richard Baker*
" tells us) who had been constant to the
" Father, notwithstanding his Faults, were
" also more tender of the Son, who was In-
" nocent, and so stuck to him, That by the Interest, chiefly of *William Marshal* Earl of *Pembroke*, who married his Aunt, they prevail'd so, that Young *Henry* was Crown'd King, yet he could not come to the Crown upon the square, but was forc'd to do Homage to Pope *Innocent* for his Kingdom of *England* and *Ireland* when he took his Coronation-Oath, and to take an Oath to pay the Church of *Rome* the Thousand Marks which his Father had granted: And though after his Coronation most of the Lords maintain'd him in his Throne, preferring their Natural Allegiance to *Henry*, before their Artificial Obligations to *Lewis*, and
Beat

Beat or Compounded the latter out of the Kingdom; yet this King *Henry*, so soon as he was got out of Protection, and came to Administer the Government himself, immediately, in gratitude, Cancels and Annuls the Charters which he had granted, on pretence (forsooth) of Minority, altho' he had taken an Oath (as well as the Legate *Guallo*, and the Protector) to restore unto the Barons of the Realm, and other his Subjects, All their Rights and Privileges; for which the Discord began between the Late King and his People: These Rights and Privileges were several times enquired into, and ascertain'd by the Returns of the Knights, who were charged to examine them; were what were enjoy'd in the time of the *Saxon* Kings, and especially under *Edward the Confessor*, and what the Charters of King *John*, and his own express'd: For 'tis ridiculous to imagine, That *William* II. *Henry* I. *Stephen*, and King *John*, should pretend to an Arbitrary Power virtually, who all came in by the Consent, if not Election, of the People. We may see how a Favourite can Absolve a King in Law and Conscience too: And what a pretty Creature a King is, when Prerogative and Humour are Synonimous, and he Acts by Advice of a single Person or Party, counter to that of his Parliament. Hence, as the Historians say, grew Storms and Tumults; no quietness to

the

the Subject, or to himself; nothing but Grievances all the long time of his Reign: He displaceth his *English* Officers to make room for Foreiners; and all the Chief Councellors, Bishops, Earls and Barons of the Kingdom are removed, as distrusted; that is, for giving him Good Counsel; and only Strangers preferred to their Places, and Honors, and Castles; the King's House and Treasury committed to their Care and Government.

These Indignities put upon the Lords, put them also upon Confederating, to reduce the King to the sense of his former Obligations; but to their Petitions he returns Dilatory and Frivolous Answers; and to requite their Favours, sends for whole Legions of *Poictavins* to Enslave the Nation; and, to crown the matter, marries himself, without Advice, to a Daughter of the Earl of *Provence*, by which he brought nothing but Poverty into this Kingdom: Afterwards, in the Long Story of this King, we hear of nothing but Grievance upon Grievance, Confederacy upon Confederacy, Parliament upon Parliament; and *Christmas* upon *Christmas*, were kept here, now there, in as many Places as he call'd his Parliaments; and to as much purpose; Bickerings upon Bickerings, and Battle upon Battle; till it grew to that height, That the

the Lords threaten'd to Expel him and his New Councels out of the Land, and to create a New King; and the Bishops threaten'd him with Excommunication; whilst, through a various Scene of Confusion and Hurly-Burly, sometimes one Party being too peremptory, sometimes t'other, with an Interchangeable undecent Shuffling on the King's Side, and a Rude Jealousy on the Lords, and various Turns of Arbitrary Fraud, and Obstinate Disputes, for above Forty Years, wherein Prerogative and Liberty grew Extravagant and Mad by turns, till the Nation was brought to the last Gasp; at length the King in the Fifty second Year of his Reign, in most solemn manner, confirms the Charters. That *Magna Charta*, which was granted in the Ninth Year, and pretended to be avoided by reason of Infancy, and the Statute of *Marlebridge*, which he had granted upon his Second Coronation in the Twentieth Year, Wherein *Magna Charta*, and *Charta de Foresta*, were confirm'd, with this Clause, *Quod contravenientes graviter puniantur*; Upon which, as is said, Peace and Tranquillity ensued: And these Charters have never since been Impugn'd or Question'd, but Confirm'd, Establish'd, and commanded to be put in Execution by Thirty two several Acts of Parliament. And from the Authority whereof, no

Man

Man ought to be permitted to recede even in his Writing, to flatter any King whatever; and Sir *Robert Filmer*, Dr. *Brady*, and Mr. *Bohun*, &c. perhaps deserv'd as severe a Correction as Collonel *Sidney*, for writing Books and Papers only, (for I do not think he deserv'd Hanging) if not greater; for their's were dispers'd by an ill-tim'd-publication, whereas t'others lay still only in his Study. We date our *Non Obstantes* from this King, which *Matthew Paris* calls an Odious and Detestable Clause, and *Roger de Thursby* with a sigh said it was a Stream deriv'd from the Sulphurious Fountain of the Clergy.

EDWARD

EDWARD I.

I Know not whether this King may come up to the Character which some of our Historians give of him in all Respects; yet, without doubt he stands an Instance and Example of Princely Qualities and Virtues fit to be imitated, and at least, as he is stiled, the Second Ornament of *Great Britain*: And as a Wise, Just and Fortunate (because Wise and Just) Prince, who in regard of his Noble Accomplishments, and Heroical and Generous Mind, deserves to be ranged amongst the Principal and Best Kings that ever were, as *Walsingham*, and *Cambden*, *Polyd. Virgil*, and Others relate. *Baker* divides his Acts into five Parts. 1. His Acts with his Temporal Lords. 2. His Acts with his Clergy. 3. With *Wales*. 4. With *Scotland*: And lastly, With *France*. And First, He gave his Lords good Contentment in the beginning of his Reign, by granting them Easier Laws, and particularly in the Statute of *Westminster*, which consists of Fifty one Chapters, and is well worth perusing. Sir *Edward Coke* says, This, and all other

Statutes

and Government of England.

Statutes made in the Reign of this King, may be ftiled by the Name of Eftablifhments, becaufe they are more Conftant, Standing, and Durable Laws, than have been made ever fince; and Sir *William Herle*, then Chief Juftice of the *Common Pleas*, fays, *Fuit le plus Sage Roy que Unques fuit.* And though thefe Laws were faid to be *Pour le Commun. profit de feint Eglife & del Realm*, yet he thought it expedient to clip the Wings of his Clergy; obferving, as is faid, their Power too predominant; and afterwards, by the Statute of *Mortmain*, kept them from ingroffing Lands, and increafing their Temporal Poffeffions; and when his Prelates preft him to repeal this Statute, he gave them for Anfwer, That it was a Statute made by the whole Body of the Realm, and therefore not in his Power, who was but one Member of that Body; not like fome of his Succeffors, who have pretended to difpenfe with all Acts of Parliaments: He united *Wales* to the Crown of *England*, partly by Force, and partly by Policy: As to his War in *Scotland*, if it were managed with the fame Policy, it had not, neverthelefs, the like fuccefs; at leaft, *Scotland* was fo unfortunate to him, that he died there: His War with *France* was but a Trifle, and foon ended in a Truce: His laft Mifunderftanding with his Lords was the Effect of

Unadvised Obstinacy on both hands; for he ought not to have insisted on sending, or their going to the Wars in *Gascoin*, without his going himself in Person; and they ought not to have refused going with him in Person, though in or out of *France* or *Scotland*; but yet he made up the Breach by his subsequent Prudence, and soft Demeanour: The worst Action of his Reign (to me) seems to be Bribing the Pope to absolve him from the Covenant made with his Subjects concerning their Charters, which he had confirm'd with an Oath; but the other good Laws which he made and observed, shall (with me) excuse one Act of Frailty or Passion. And if he be censured for his Taxes, he is, in part, justified by his well bestowing them, to his own Honour, and Good of his Kingdom.

EDWARD

EDWARD II.

WE are not to expect much good from a King who begins his Reign with the breach of his Father's Admonitions, and the Obligations he lay under by him in matters of Duty; Commands which his Father gave him in charge with his last Words, on pain of a Curse for his Disobedience, as *Stow* says. And here it may be observed, how wretched and contemptible a Creature (pardon the Expression) even a King (as well as another Man) is, when he hath once broke loose from the Principles of Honour and Morality; when the Natural Bonds of Modesty are unhinged and broken: How he wavers and shuffles, and is driven about by every Wind, that he cannot be steady to himself, or any one else. When Men have once forsaken the Path of Vertue, they walk in an endless Maze; they can't rely on themselves, and therefore are impos'd upon, and misled by every one. For when a Man cannot justify himself to himself, he can never do it to another; and Kings generally stand so much upon the Prerogative

tive of being like Gods, that they scorn to be thought to be in the wrong, like Men.

Here we may see how fatal 'tis to prefer a private Person, before the Publick; and for a Prince to espouse the Interest of a Favourite, so far as to put him in competition with all his other Subjects; and to oppose his Welfare to theirs.

The whole Reign of this Poor King is but one Farce of Folly and Misfortune; contemn'd by his Subjects, and even by his own Wife, who revenged upon him the violation of a double Tye of Obedience: This was the immediate, as well as natural Consequence, of relying upon the Opinion and Advice of single Persons, contrary to the Counsels, and against the Advice of the Wisdom of the Nation. After Troubles on the behalf of *Gaveston*; Troubles in *Scotland*, with a faint ill-managed War; Troubles on account of the *Spencers*; Troubles in his own Family, (for he was no wiser in his Oeconomicks than his Politicks) with his Wife, &c. he was at last shamefully Deposed, barbarously Used, and villanously Murther'd. A Person in his Natural Capacity certainly to be lamented, as having some Virtues and Good Qualities: Fit to make an Accomplish't Gentleman, though not a Good King.

Kingly

Kingly Government did not seem to be his Talent, for he lived as if born for himself, not for others; and there is certainly a difference in the Quality of governing a Man's self and others, between governing and being govern'd. To this purpose I must bring in *Montaign*, who seems to have a good Notion of the Thing. " Doubtless, " says he, it can be no easy Task to Rule " others, when we find it so hard a matter to " govern our selves: And as to the Thing " Dominion, which seems so charming, the " Frailty of Human Wisdom, and the Dif- " ficulty in Choice of Things that are New, " and Doubtful to us, consider'd, I'm very " much of Opinion, That it is far more " pleasant to follow, than to lead; and that " it is a great Settlement and Satisfaction of " Mind, to have only one Path to walk " in, and to have none to answer for but a " Man's self: For without doubt (says he) " there is a great and painful Duty incum- " bent upon a Good King: How much " doth it import Kings to have a Good Ad- " vice of Counsel? For, I doubt we shall find but few Kings (whether of God Almighty's making, or our own, *i. e.* whether by Inheritance *(Solus Deus facit hæredes)* or Election) of *Cyrus*'s Qualifications, who says, *That no Man is fit to Rule, but he who in his own Worth is of greater value than all those he is to govern.*

E 3 *EDWARD*

EDWARD III.

THE Reign of *Edward* the Third was more a School of Arms than Civil Polity: For having in the beginning patch'd up an Indifferent Peace with *Scotland*, he is immediately embroil'd in a War with *France*, with which, and some few Matters in *Scotland*, he was engaged all his Life-time. It is true, in his Parliament at *Westminster*, Supply and Grievances were pretty warmly Debated: And he has his weak Side in the Business of *Alice Peirce* his Concubine; but I let this pass as a Failing: (And who is without some?) But when he was at leisure he made Good Laws, and particularly in the Affair of Purveying: He caus'd all Pleas to be in *English*, that the Subjects might understand the Laws; Ordain'd Sumptuary Laws, *&c.* and in the general was a Great and Good Prince; as *Walsingham*; *Fuerat nempe Rex iste, inter omnes Reges Orbis & Principes, Gloriosus, Benignus, Clemens & Magnificus: Belliger fuit insignis & fortunatus, qui de Cunctis Congressibus*

gressibus & in Terra & Mare semper triumphali gloriâ Victoriam Reportavit. I can only attribute this to the Character *Stow* gives of him, *viz.* That he advanced Persons to Dignities for Merit only, and who did excel others in Innocency of Life.

RICHARD II.

SOME Princes have Erred upon a mistaken Consideration, some through a wilful and rash Inconsideration; some have taken Measures by Advice of Friends (as they thought) and have been deceived by Misrepresentations; (these may be pittied); Others have Miscarried by hearkening only to Minions and Favourites, are headstrong, and resolvedly deaf and obstinate against Advice: But the Actions and Conduct of this King are so Unaccountable, that it would puzzle a *Matchiavel* to assign him a Character, or to fix him in any Rule or Principle of Government, Good or Bad. The Rebellion of *John*, or *Wat Tyler*, ought not to be laid at his Door; it is called an Accident, though it had some dismal Effects in it; but the occasion which appears, was the Abuse of a Collector who gathered the Poll-Money; yet it may teach Kings, that it is a ticklish and dangerous Experiment to let out a Revenue or Tax to Farm; so that it may be screwed up into what may be called in the Country Oppression. This King's first Misun-

Misunderstanding, in earnest, or Misdemeanor, if I may so speak, after his coming to Age, was imposed upon him by way of Surprise, and Artificial Insinuation of Favourites; it might be the result of a hot Indiscretion, not of a premeditated Violence or Invasion of Ill-natur'd Policy: And if the Duke of *Ireland*, *Michael de la Pool*, the Chancellor, or the Archbishop of *York*, were in fault on the one side, neither was the Duke of *Gloucester*, the Bishop of *Ely*, &c. to be altogether excused, on the other; and the Parliament imposing on the King Thirteen Lords to have oversight under the King, as they called it, was an unsufferable Encroachment on the Spirit of a Young Prince: And he had reason to have recourse to the Judges for their Opinions and Directions touching what had passed in that Parliament as to their Participation of the Government with him; whose Opinion (though they had the misfortune to suffer for it) was not so Illegal, but Justifiable by the Laws, saving only in Two or Three of the Questions to which they gave their Answers. But Law is not always measured by its own Rule, it stands or falls according to the Circumstance of Times: A Man may at some time sooner and better Steal a Horse (as they say) than look on at others. This first Affront so put

upon

upon the King, gave him a prejudice to Parliaments ever after, and consequently put him upon indirect Means and Practices to Debauch the Constitution; and we may be sure Kings will never want Tools fit for their purpose. Hence were conceived those prejudices also against the Duke of *Glocester* and the other Lords; the King had Reason to be out of Tuition when he came to be of full Age: 'Tis true, the Attempting of the Duke of *Glocester*'s Life in that Treacherous manner, was not to be excused; neither was his Behaviour to be pardoned towards the King; he reproached him too severely on all Occasions, for though he was the King's Uncle, he was not always to be his Governor; they were both in Fault, no doubt, and both equally Unfortunate in their End. 'Twas an unhappy Reign, divided between too haughty Subjects, and Ill-designing Favourites, too powerful for a Young Inconsiderate King to Manage with Prudence and equal Power. Whether Chief Justice *Tresilian* did according to Law or not, 'tis certain his Death was not according to Law; and as the Duke of *Glocester* had taken his Life, so his own was soon after taken away without Trial also, in an Arbitrary manner: And the Earl of *Arundel* had the same Measure he meeted to *Calvery*, one of the Queens Esquires. The Banishing the

the Duke of *Norfolk*, and *Hereford*, and the Archbishop of *Canterbury*, was rather a fault in the Politicks of those times (for it seems it was the Custom then to Punish the Faults of Great Men only with Banishment, but an ill-advised Custom,) than want of Consideration in the King. Sir *John Busby*, the Speaker of Parliament, was the most in fault, in attributing Vain, and almost Blasphemous Titles to the King; Titles fitter (as is observed) for the Majesty of God; and putting him upon a piece of Omnipotence, in Recalling his Pardons; which the Lords, Spiritual and Temporal, Adjudged in the Affirmative, That the King might Revoke; but the Lawyers and Judges, having been burnt before, designed to give Judgment t'other way, and had no mind to Determine of Transactions in Parliament any more, nor of the Kings Prerogative in such Ticklish Times: Though at the next Parliament at *Chester*, the Judges were drawn in to give another Extraordinary Judgment, *viz.* " That when Articles are propounded by " the King, to be handled in Parliament, " that if other Articles are handled be-" fore those are determined, it is Trea-" son in them that do it." What was there Extravagant that was not done in this Parliament? He brought it about, as the History says, That he obtained the
whole

whole Power of the Parliament to be Conferred upon certain few Perſons; who proceeded to Conclude upon many things which concerned generally the things of the whole Parliament, to the great Prejudice of the State, and dangerous Example in time to come. What could we expect from a King who was Taught, That the Laws of the Realm were in his Head and his Breaſt? By reaſon of which fantaſtical Opinion, he Deſtroyed Noblemen, and Impoveriſhed the Commons; which was one of the Articles againſt him; and which was much ſuch a worthy fancy as *Wat Tyler* had, who putting his Hand to his Lips, ſaid, Before Four Days come to an End, all the Laws of *England* ſhould proceed from his Mouth. But I am weary of the Medley of this King's Story: In ſhort, if we ſurvey him in his Taxations, in his Laws and Ordinances after all, and in the Station of a Chriſtian, and Man, as well as King; we ſhall, with a little Charity, or good Nature, conclude him Blameable rather by Accident than natural Temper: And as to his Conditions, That they were more the Fault of his Education than Inclination; and at the bottom, thoſe Failings that were in him, retained the tincture of the light Inconſtancy of his Mother. He is another unfortunate Inſtance of the Inſtability

ſtability and Miſery of a King when he leaves the Track of Law and Juſtice, for the Ways of Humour and Paſſion. Sir *Robert Cotton* Obſerves, " That *Buſby*'s " Contrivance of Compounding with De- "linquents, wrought ſuch Diſtaſte in the " Affections of the People, that it grew " the Death of the One, and Depoſition " of the Other.

HENRY

HENRY IV.

IN the next Six Reigns, during the Divisions of the Houses of *York* and *Lancaster*, the Kingdom was scarce ever cool enough for Observations of Civil Polity and Administration. The Thirteen Years of this King were divided between Conspiracies and Wars. And as he came to the Crown without a Title, with respect to *Richard* II. or the Earl of *Marsh*, who had the Undoubted Right, as being of the Eldest House; without any Title, unless what he had from the People, (or, as *Stow* says, was Ordained King more by Force than lawful Succession, or Election), so he held it in continued Trouble and Confusion, saving only the last Year: And 'tis said, he was well pleased that there were always Troubles that there might be no Calm or Interval for Reflection. He was so jealous of his Crown, that in his Sickness he would have it laid by him upon his Bolster, for fear some body should Dispossess him of it, as he had *Richard* the II[d]; and his Son as readily took it up, for fear of some other Interposition. Though he had not leisure for Politicks, yet he he made a very useful Observation, fit to be thought on by Kings, *viz.* " That of *Eng-lishmen,* so long as they have Wealth, so long shalt thou have Obeysance; but when they are Poor, they are always ready to make Insurrection at every motion. Here we have also a great Example of a King's Son submitting to the Laws, and of a King protecting and countenancing a Judge in a due Execution of them; and also of a Judge with a steady Gravity and Resolution putting the Ancient Laws of the Realm in Execution, without Favour or Partiality.

HENRY

HENRY V.

THE Reign of this King was wholly taken up with the Wars in *France*; and here may be seen what an *English* Prince can do, when he himself is Brave and Generous, and stands well in the Opinion of his Subjects; they paid him Homage before he was Crown'd, and voluntarily granted him a Subsidy without asking; and he, on the other hand, ask'd but few: By which it appears (as Sir *Richard Baker* observes) what great matters a moderate Prince may do, and yet not grieve his Subjects with Taxations. Under this King, who was of *English* true Honour, the Honour of the Nation was at the highest Character; for in a Councel holden at *Constance*, it was Decreed, That *England* should have the Title of the *English* Nation, and should be accounted one of the Five Principal Nations in Rank before *Spain*; which often before had been moved, but never till then Granted.

HENRY VI.

I Know not what to say to the Reign of this unfortunate King, only that it is an instance of the Impertinence of Fortune, and of the Unsteadiness of Human Affairs; although *Philip de Comines* says, he was a very Silly Man, and almost an Innocent; yet this silly Innocence seems to be what we call Simplicity in the modest acceptation of the word, and the Effect rather of Choice, or Observation, than Defect. 'Tis true he had a sort of Passive Understanding; but he had Judgment enough to distinguish Good and Bad, between Virtue and Vice, Success and Misfortune; to resent these as a Man, but overlook them as a Christian, and what Sir *Francis Bacon* reports of him upon the account of his being to be Canonized, (That the Pope, who was jealous of his Honour and of the Dignity of the See of *Rome*, knowing that *Henry* the VIth was reputed in the World abroad but for a Simple Man, was afraid it would but diminish the Estimation of that kind of Honour, if there were not a distance kept between Innocents and Saints,) seems to be brought in rather for the sake of the Jingle or Jest, than Truth. His greatest symptom of Weakness was suffering a Wife to be imposed upon him, and then being ever after imposed upon by that Wife; but I doubt this may have been the condition of some Wise Men; and the Earl of *Suffolk* plaid the fool in the Match, not the King, any otherwise than by taking the Advice of a single Person, without, and contrary to the Counsel of his Other Peers, *&c.* And what have Wiser Kings done, beset with a Favourite or a Wife? Whereas he had both; which shews, that 'tis not so much a King's personal and private Wisdom, as That of the General Council of a Nation, is to be relied on. The Ill-advised Tragedy of the Duke of *Glocester* made Room and open'd way for That of the King's, by letting in the Duke of *York*'s pretensions to the Crown, and soon ended in the Death of the Duke of *Suffolk* himself. So unsafe is it for any Favourite, how Great soever, to presume on his Own strength against the Interest and Policy of the Commonwealth. The Other Affairs of this Reign seem transacted upon a stage of Fortune or Fate, rather than Prudence or Policy, trod between a Headstrong People, Ambitious Nobles, and a Queen too apt to Rule, and a King too easy and apt to Suffer

If we may learn any thing from this Reign, 'tis only this, That Virtue and Goodness, without Policy and Justice, nor Policy without Virtue and Resolution, can Establish a Throne: But after all, Fate it self seems to weigh down the Scale; his Father's Prophecy (is said) was not to be avoided, which I leave in the Words of *Howard's Defensative against the Poyson of supposed Prophesies*, viz. "What Prophet could have picked out of "*Mars* and *Saturn* the manifold Mishaps "which befel the Prince of Blessed Memo-"ry, King *Henry* the VIth; sometimes Sleep-"ing in a Port of Honour, sometimes Float-"ing in the Surges of Mishap; sometimes "Possessing Foreign Crowns, sometimes "Spoiled and Deprived of his Own; some-"times a Prince, sometimes a Prisoner; some-"times in plight to give Succour to the Mise-"rable, sometimes a Fugitive amongst the "Desperate. *Habington* in his History of *Edward* the IVth says, That this poor King in so many Turns and Vicissitudes, never met with one fully to his Advantage. And *Cambden* says, He was Four times taken Prisoner; and in the End Despoiled both of his Kingdom and Life.

EDWARD IV.

THE first Twelve Years of this King's Reign (if I may so call it, who came to the Kingdom. (as *Biondi* says) not by Power or Justice, but by the People's Inclination) were passed in a ferment of Blood, and the better part of his Two and twenty (if I may so say) were taken up in Wars and Executions; not so much occasioned by *Henry* the VIth as by the Earl of *Warwick*; so dangerous a thing it is to put an Affront upon a powerful Subject: But especially King *Edward* shewed a very weak part in this Management, who came to the Crown chiefly by the Earl of *Warwick's* Interest, and with a *confessed Election* of his People, when he had Married a Subject of no great Parentage or Interest, to disoblige such a Subject, Dishonourably, who had so great a Stroke and made such a Figure in the Nation. But all Rules of Policy, they say, must submit to Love; therefore to pass that Oversight, for which there is an Excuse made: Certainly the Confidence and Trust afterwards by him repos'd in the Duke of *Glocester*, was a manifest Infatuation, not to be supported

ed with any pretence of common Consideration, or colour of Reason. And though *Philip de Comines* says he was the Goodliest
Personage, yet I doubt he was not the Wisest,
and he might well affirm that his Master
Lewis of *France* exceeded *Edward* the IVth
in Sense and Wisdom. How idle and viti-
ous was his Consideration upon that imagined Prophecy, That *G.* should Dispossess
his Children of the Crown; to suffer it to
influence him so far, as to consent to the
Murther (as 'tis said) of *G.* Duke of *Clarence*, on supposition (foreign enough) that
That *G.* was intended him; whereas it fell
out to be *Glocester*; to whose Tyranny he
left them by this Foolish and Ungodly Fancy,
and such a prophane extravagant Application of Sorceries; to which, in truth, that
Age was every where too much addicted.
And 'twas not his jealous practices with the
Duke of *Britaign*, against *Henry* Earl of
Richmond, could secure the Crown to his
Children, when he overlook'd the more immediate Danger.

EDWARD V.

ONE would have thought *Edward* IV. might have, without Sorcery or Prophecy, foreseen what would become of the committing the Care of *Edward* the Vth to his Brother the Duke of *Glocester*, who had before Killed *Henry* the VIth with his own Hand, in all probability without Commandment or Knowledge of his Brother and his Son, in his own presence; and was suspected also to have a hand in the Death of his other Brother the Duke of *Clarence*; besides the symptom of an ill-contrived Soul and Body: Without taking notice of all the villanous popular Harangues, Insinuations and Artifices used by the Duke of *Glocester*, to get the King's Person into his Power, out of the Hands of the Queen and her Friends. In short, this poor Prince was an Unhappy instance of a misplaced Guardianship, and an Unnatural Uncle's Care. A Youth, made a Jest of Sovereignty for Ten Weeks, and Sacrificed to Ambition at Eleven Years of Age; and an instance of the fatal Credulity of a Woman, too apt to be deceived as well as to deceive: He and his poor Brother

were

were Murthered in the *Tower*, Betrayed by an Uncle, and too easily delivered up by a Mother. A Reign, a fit Subject only for Poetry.

Twin-Brethren by their Death, What had they (done? *Aleyn*
  Oh Richard *sees a Fault that they were in!* *Hist. of*
It is not Actual, but a Mortal One, *Hen. VII.*
  They Princes were, 'twas their Original Sin.

Why should so sweet a Pair of Princes lack
Their Innocents Day *i'th'* English Almanack?

F   RICHARD

RICHARD III.

THIS ―― was so great a Monster in all Respects, that he ought not (for the Honour of *England*) to have place amongst the Catalogue of Kings. There ought to be nothing Recorded of him, but only this, That he died in the Field with his Sword in his Hand. 'Tis said, he made Good Laws; but I know of none Extraordinary, but only One, which is rather a Popular Declaration of what was so before; and that was, That the Subjects of this Realm shall not be charged by any Benevolence, or such like Charge, but it shall be damn'd and annull'd for ever. Let his Laws be transferr'd to another Reign; let us not acknowledge Mercy from the Hands of Blood. Sir *Francis Bacon* saith, " That his Good Laws were
" but the Brocage of an Usurper, thereby to
" win the hearts of the People, as being Con-
" scious to himself, that the true Obligations
" of Sovereignty in him failed: And if he
" had lived, no doubt, would have proved
" such a One as King *James* the First de-
" scribes a Tyrant to be.

HENRY VII.

IT behoved *Henry* the Seventh, having in himself but a slim sort of distant Title, to support himself by Policy: And here will appear what Single Prudence can do: This maintain'd his Crown, whilst he trim'd between Conquest, Military Election, Parliamentary, Birth, Donation, and Marriage: Though he did not care to be beholding to the Last, and to take a precarious Right from a Wife. Sir *Walter Rawleigh* says, "He was a Politick Prince, "who by the Engine of his Wisdom beat "down and overturn'd as many Strong "Oppositions both before and after he "wore the Crown, as ever King of *Eng-* "*gland* did. And *Cambden*, Through whose "Care, Vigilancy, and Policy, and Fore-"casting Wisdom for times to come, the "State and Commonwealth of *England* "hath to this day stood Established and "Invincible; *Henricus noster Septimus cum* "*omnes Regni recte Administrandi Artes* "*calleret, sic his Ornamentis Instructus venit* "*ut cum Pacem Exulantem, Exul, exterrem-* "*que Extorris concomitatus esset, reducem quo-* "*que,*

"*que, Redux aportaret. Win. Com. de rebus Brit.*

But, perhaps, the Tyranny of his Predeceffor might make his firſt Steps more eaſy: However, I take *Henry* the Seventh's Maſter-piece of Wiſdom to be, That he uſed That of other Mens alſo: He call'd his Parliament, and conſulted with it upon all Occaſions, eſpecially when he had any Provocations to War from *France* or *Scotland*: Not inſiſting on, but ever waving that impertinent piece of Prerogative, of Declaring War upon a King's own Head: This Method open'd his Subjects Purſes; This procured even a Benevolence as odious as it had been heretofore, and Great Sums of Money were ſoon collected by it: The Commotions which happen'd in the *North* and *Weſt* upon gathering the Subſidies, were but ſlight Exceptions, taken on the Occaſion of the Extravagancies and Paſſions of particular Perſons: And the Buſineſs of *Lambert Simnell*, and the greater Attempt of *Perkin Warbeck*, were but the Effect of a Woman's Malice, and promoted by the Dutcheſs of *Burgundy*, who was an Avowed Enemy to the Houſe of *Lancaſter*. Sir *Francis Bacon* tells us, "His Time did "excel for Good Commonwealth Laws; ſo "that he may be juſtly celebrated for the "Beſt Law-giver to this Nation, after King "*Edward*

' Edward the First. For his Laws, whoso
' marks them well, are deep, and not
' Vulgar; not made upon the Spur of a
' particular Occasion for the present, but
' out of providence for the future, to make
' the State of his People still more and more
' happy, after the manner of the Legisla-
' tors in Ancient and Heroical Times. I suppose he means the State-Laws against Retainers and Riots; these seem more properly to be made on his own Account, and that no Person assisting a King *de Facto* should be attainted therefore by course of Law, or Act of Parliament; and that if any such Act should be made, it should be void, which seems also calculated for a particular purpose (though it hath since made so much noise in the World) [as the Act to take away the Writ *De Hæretico Combu-rendo*, was in King *Charles* the Second's Time.] And this *de Facto* Act seems to have no foundation at that time, unless it were for fear of the Earl of *Warwick*, who was the last Heir-Male of the *Plantagenets*; for the King and People most certainly knew, that *Richard*, the Younger Brother of *Edward* the Fifth, was Dead, and Safe, whom *Perkin* pretended to represent: And methinks, after all, this Act seems to have but a Weak and Dishonourable Foundation, and leaves an ill Savour, and will cast a Reflection some-where: For Fears and Jealousies put

Men

Men and Kings too often upon poor-spirited Actions. But letting this pass; Another touch of his over-Wisdom, *viz.* his Disposition to squeeze Money out of his Subjects Purses by Forfeitures on Penal Laws, was an Excess of Policy scarce to be excused; and, as is said, without all doubt proved the Blot of his Time; and as Sir *Robert Cotton* observes, There is no string will sooner jarr in the Commonwealth than this, if it be generally touched. This was that which passed for the Disgrace of his Reign, though what may pass under the Name of Severe Justice: And though he escaped the Violent Consequences of it himself, yet the fatal Return overtook *Empson* and *Dudley* in the beginning of the next Reign, who were both executed for Treason, for extending this *Summum Jus* to Violence and Injury, and turning Law and Justice into Rapin; (Though it will puzzle a Lawer to determine what Species of Treason this is, unless it be against the Laws, by traiterously betraying the Trust reposed in them). But no Government, King, or Person, is without some Failing, and Wisdom it self may be overacted.

HENRY

HENRY VIII.

I Am not to determine how it came about, yet it may be observable, That though this King came to the Crown by an Undoubted Right of Succession, as Heir of the House of *Lancaster* by his Father, and of the House of *York* by his Mother; yet upon his Coronation the People were ask'd, Whether they would receive him for their King? But I know this will be thought a trivial Matter of Form, not worth taking notice of. It is said his first Years were a Reign by Book, having come from the Instruction and Contemplation of Good, to Action; his Notions stuck by him some Years: And not to pretend to single Sufficience at those Years, at least, That he might know how to perform his Coronation-Oath, he chose a Wise Councel to direct him in the Observation of the Laws; and as they generally do in all New Reigns, He redress'd the Grievances of the former, by making Examples of the Oppressors in the last. He did not enter into the War with *France* upon his own Head, neither upon the Advice of his Privy Council; but

but had it debated in Parliament, where it was resolved, That Himself with a Royal Army should invade *France*; and then for that purpose an Extraordinary Subsidy was willingly granted towards the Charges thereof: these were the beginnings of his Reign; and he might have finish'd it with the same Honour and Wisdom, if *Woolsey* had not piously told him, He might lay aside the use of his Understanding, and his own Consideration (no doubt to rely on his): That he should not need to trouble himself with frequenting the Council-Table, but might take his Pleasure, &c. (Admirable Councel for a Priest)! And he himself would give him Information, &c. Thus he ingrossed the King, disobliged the King's Friends, caus'd the Archbishop of *Canterbury*, Bishop of *Winchester*, Dukes of *Norfolk* and *Suffolk*, to withdraw from Court, and Topp'd his Prerogative upon the King's, and led him away by the Misdirections of his own False Oracle; persuades and puts the King upon Lending the Emperor Money, who was poor and Insolvent; because, forsooth, the *French* King had withheld the Revenue of the Bishop of *Tourney*, that is, his Own. After he had tired the People with his Civil Justice before, he sets up for an Arbitrary Spiritual Power in himself: Obtains an Office from the Pope to dispence with Offences against Spiritual

ritual Laws, and erects a Trade for Sin, to make Virtue and Religion Venial, and betrays the King into the Restoring or Surrendring *Tourney*, for great Gifts, and greater Promises, after that he found it did not turn to Account, and he could make nothing of it by way of Yearly Income: And thus dishonour'd the King and Nation, and like a very Godly Prelate, dissolv'd the King and Court into all sort of Luxury, and the Priesthood it self into Licentiousness and Disorder: And so far the Artificial Malice and Villany of this Sawcy and Bloody Butcher's Son went, who had neither Honour or Religion, That he persuaded the King to sacrifice his Nobility to him, and the Duke of *Buckingham* must be made an Example and Martyr to his Revenge, for only pouring a little Water into his Shooes, when he had the Impudence to dip his Hands in the Bason, whilst the Duke held it to the King to wash. He alone could create Misunderstandings between the King, Lords and Commons, by vertue of his Lies and Misrepresentations of Matters from one to the other, altho' he had been caught in them more than once: He dissolv'd Convocations, by vertue of his Power Legantine, which were convok'd by the Archbishop; and calls Him and all the Clergy to another Place, according to his own Imperious Fancy; diverts

verts the Laws of the Land, and seeks to raise Money by Commission, which the People opposed, and the King was afterwards forced to Disclaim: On the other hand abuses the King's Grace, and takes it upon himself; alters the State of the King's House, Retrenches the Allowance of his Servants; and in short, arrogates the Power over Servants, and Master also, and assumes the Power and Honour of the King, and Stiles and Directs *Ego & Rex meus* in his Writings and Letters to *Rome*, and Foreign Parts: This could an humble Successor of the Apostles do? And by the bye, It may be worth observing, how far Pride can inspire these Prelatical Sparks with Presumption, who pretend to be but the Representatives of the Apostles, to exalt themselves above, and Lord it over Kings, whom yet they themselves acknowledge to represent God: I regard not their Distinctions, neither before nor since their Compliment of the Supremacy, which they would resume if they could, without a Pope. But it happen'd the Cardinal carried on the Scene and State of Pageantry too far, even to his own Ruin; and the King's Eyes were open'd at length, after that the Cardinal had cut him out a way for the Ruin, or Reformation rather of the Church, as well as himself; and by his Exorbitant Behaviour had open'd the Door to the Parliament

and Government of England.

ment to Redress the Grievances, and provide for a Remedy against them, by restraining and wholsome Laws. I am the more particular upon this Prelate, because he was the Hinge upon which every thing turn'd; and would set a Mark upon him for Kings to know whom to avoid, and for what Reasons: And would upon all Occasions also remind them how wretched and inconsiderable a Creature a King is, when he abdicates his own Reason, to submit it to another's; and waves the Publick, for any private Whispers of Admonition.

I desire to be excused from medling with the long Story of the King's Quarrel with the Pope, and the Occasion; and shall pass over the Alterations in Religion in this King's time; or what was more considerable, the Change and Dissolution of Religious Houses: I have nothing to do with his Shifting and Dissolving of Wives neither: There are particular Histories of the Reformation enow, and fresh in every one's Memory; having had an occasion, not long since, to review them, and consider them afresh. There are Plays and Novels also of the other to gratify the Female Politicians; who, whether they ought to be severe upon him, or not, I know not, and leave to them to determine: This is besides my Design, as being out of all Ordinary Rules of Civil Policy: Therefore waving all Enquiry into the Reasons or Provocations of one or t'other, though I know some are assign'd and remark'd to his Disadvantage, others to his Advantage; I shall dismiss my self with this general Remark upon the Qualities of a Man, or King; That when Either have once broke through the first Obligations of Justice or Virtue, he makes but little difficulty in the proceeding upon Attempts of the same Nature: Though after all, to speak impartially, and without Reflection, I am not satisfied, but the first Occasion of Divorce, and Reformation too, was in its self justifiable, though the Circumstances inducing it are suspected; and it was concluded a Reason sought, not offer'd. But certainly Sir *Walter Raleigh*'s Character o[f] him is not to be justified, who says "That if all the Pictures and Patern[s]" "of a Merciless Prince were lost in th[e]" "World, they might all again be paint"-"ed to the life out of the Story of thi[s]" "King: And that of Sir *Robert Naunto*[n] is as ill-natur'd; viz. "Having a Desig[n]" "to marry within the Degrees Unlaw"-"fu

"ful, he set his Learned Men at work
"to prove it lawful; and after a while,
"being cloy'd, and desiring Change, set
"them again on work to prove it unlaw-
"ful; He never spared Man in his An-
"ger, or Woman in his Lust: This is Sa-
tyrically said, but not truly; For he had
no mind to marry at first where he did,
but did it in Obedience to his Father's
Will, and against the Grain with himself: And he liv'd with this first Wife
Twenty Years, and never took notice of
the Unlawfulness of that Marriage, till
it was objected against him again, and
the President of *Paris* started and moved
it on the Proposal of Marriage between
the Lady *Mary* (his Daughter by *Ka-
therine*) and the Duke of *Orleance*, the
second Son to the *French* King: And as
to the Cruelty towards Men, the Death
of the Lord *Cromwell*, and that of the
Duke of *Norfolk*'s Son, *Henry* Earl of
Surry, found most of Severity; yet as to
the first, he had rais'd him from a Smith's
Son, he was Cardinal *Woolsey*'s Pupil, and
trod in his Steps: He was Attainted by Parliament, and the Record says, for Crimes of
Heresy and Treason, perhaps the Advice of
the Match with the Lady *Ann* of *Cleve*;
but I think it doth not argue Cruelty in
the King neither towards him or her:

He dismiss'd her with a gentle Farewel after her Marriage was declared Unlawful by the Convocation, and adjudged so in Parliament; and she lived sixteen Years after, and died in the Fourth Year of Queen *Mary*: As to the other, It is plain it was not to gratify his Personal Cruelty: For being no Lord of Parliament, he was Arraigned at *Guildhall* before a Special Commission, and found guilty by a Jury; the Charge of bearing Arms which belonged to the King and Prince, may seem somewhat slight; yet it is always dangerous to play with Edged Tools, and the *Ragion di stato* may in part excuse it. In the main he appears a King of a great deal of Honour, not without a Good-natur'd Generosity: He was careful also to maintain the Civil Constitution, and devout to the Privileges of Parliament: He carried it fair with his Subjects in the general, and was never Ill-natur'd or Froward (as far as I can perceive) without some Colour of Justice. I know not whether I can justify him in his Politicks so well, in his contradicting by the Will, the Disposition of the Crown, and its Succession, which he had before Established in Parliament; especially to bring in Queen *Mary*, after his Subjects had sworn to the Parliamentary Succession of his Daughter *Elizabeth*:

Elizabeth: Besides, That this was subsequently by Implication, to affirm the Legitimacy of his Mariage with *Katharine* of *Spain*, which was with so much Solemnity laboured, and declared Unlawful: All that can be said, is, That he might, in respect to the Mother, be unwilling to suffer the Daughter to be Bastardised: And we always ought to construe the Actions of Princes *in mitiori sensu*, and to take them by the best part of the Handle in History: To speak well of them, if we can any ways justify it; and to be silent in Doubtful Characters, if we cannot Commend.

EDWARD VI.

I Am at a loss in speaking to the Short Reign of *Edward* the Sixth: He seems born and design'd for the Advancement of Ecclesiastical and Civil Polity, and to be snatched away to the Disappointment of Human Expectations; to intimate, That there is no Establishment of Happiness to be relied on here below. However, that Government which might have come to something in himself, was Unfortunate in the Administration of the Councel which his Father with so much Care had assign'd him, and impertinently enough shuffled between the Aspiring Conduct of the Great Men, and the Foolish Ambition of Pretending Women: These interrupted the Wisdom of Councels (though the Protector did his part well enough at first, till he came to pull down a Church, and two Bishops Houses in the *Strand*, to make him a Mansion-House, &c.) For after the Disturbances of the Nation on the Account of Religion, and the Inclosures at Home, and with relation to the

French

French and *Scots* Abroad, had been managed with Prudence and Honour, and the Kingdom began to appear with a Face of Peace and Satisfaction: How vain are Mortal Considerations! Behold the whole Oeconomy is on a sudden Discomposed, and the Frame of Government Subverted: And a Frivolous Pretence of Place between two Women Unhinges the Constitution, and first exposes, and then destroys and ruins the Husbands, by vertue of the False Designs of a Third Person behind the Curtain, who grafted Villany artificially upon their Follies, and at last, as was suspected, brought in the King himself, whose Death also is laid at the same Door. What the Sense of our Neighbours was concerning it, you may read in *Mezeray*:
" *France* and *England* held pretty good
" Correspondence, when Death cut the
" Thread of Young King *Edward*'s Days;
" It was believ'd to proceed from a flow
" Poyson, and *John Dudley*, Duke of *Nor-*
" *thumberland*, was suspected guilty of the
" Crime, he having suggested to him to
" Institute *Jane* of *Suffolk* for Heiress to the
" Crown: However it were, it prov'd a Fatal Policy to the poor Lady *Jane* and himself too. I confess, I cannot see why *Edward* the Sixth might not make bold with *Mary*, as well as his Father had done before

fore him, and difpofe of the Crown by Will, as he did; efpecially for the Propagating and Eftablifhing the Infant Reformation, if that Age had been ferious, and well agreed in the Bufinefs of Religion: For we fhall find, I doubt, in Hiftory (notwithftanding all Obfervation to the contrary), That if Religion be not fupported by State-props, it will not ftand long; and that That which hath only for its Ingredients Mercy and Honour, will be in fhort time overrun, and go to the Walls, whilft the Religion of Violence and Blood will propagate it felf by Inquifitions, and the Artifices of its own pretended Zeal. And that, notwithftanding all Innocent Precautions, 'tis too true, That a Prince of *Matchiavell*'s Compofition, will at prefent, and for once, prevail over one of a Sincere Vertue, and open Honour : This, I fay, upon the appearing Reafon of the thing, That our Nation in particular may not be impofed upon over and over again with the fame Appearances, and only that we fhould ftand upon our Guard againft all Popifh Reprefentations, how innocently foever colour'd; and againft all Foreign Overtures, how well foever baited.

Queen *MARY*.

ONE would have thought, that the Reign of this Queen might have satisfied a Nation (of any Capacity of Thinking) in the Professions of a Papist, and what weight the Promises of the Church of *Rome* to Hereticks ought to have with Protestants. The Principles and Practices of Papists were well enough known, even in those times, in our Neighbouring Country of *France* under *Henry* the II^d, by the Execution of so great a Number of Protestants, who were Burn'd in the *Greve*, the common Place of Execution; but the manner of it was not Common: "They were Haled up by a "Pully and Iron Chain, then suffered to "fall down in the midst of a great "Fire; which was repeated several times: "And 'tis said, the King himself would "needs feed his own Eyes with this "Tragical and Melancholy Spectacle, "and that the Horrible and Mournful "Shreiks of one of those poor Wretches "left so lively an Impression in his Ima-
"gination,

"gination, that all his Life long he had
" from time to time a very frightful
" and terrible Remembrance of those
" dreadful Groans: However it were,
" it is certain that the Smell of those
" Carcasses then Roasted, got into the
" Brains of a great many People; who
" on the one hand beholding the (false)
" Constancy, as *Mezeray* calls it, and on
" the other hand the scandalous dissolute
" Living, named this Justice (as he
" terms it) a Persecution, and their Pu-
" nishment a Martyrdom. This is the
tender Account given of it by a *Popish*
Historian. And he says, " Faggots were
" then lighted every where against the
" Protestants. Queen *Mary* made her
passage to the Throne through her Promises to the *Norfolk* and *Suffolk* Gentlemen, that she would make no Alterations in Religion; but before she was
warm in it, she shewed how she dissembled her false Favours, and removed
the Protestant Bishops, and sent *Cran-
mer* the Archbishop of *Canterbury*, and
Latimer, and others, to the *Tower*, and
passed Judgment on them to Dye: All
this before her Coronation. And as
Mezeray tells us, " When she was once
" Absolute Mistress, she Cemented the
" Throne with the Blood of the Lady
" *Jane,*

"*Jane*, her Husband, her Father, and almoſt all her Kindred, and after that ſhe ſpilt much more to Reſtore the Catholick Religion; which brought the State into ſuch Convulſions as had like to have proved Mortal, and all for the Advantage of a ſhort Duration. Thus *Mezeray* ſtill, a *French* and *Popiſh* Writer. And, in truth, the Lady *Elizabeth* eſcaped very narrowly; for *Gardiner*, that ſpecial Biſhop of *Winchester*, had procured her to be ſent to Priſon, and had framed a Warrant under certain Councellors Hands to put her to Death; but that Mr. *Bridges*, Lieutenant of the *Tower*, pitying her Caſe, went to the Queen to know her Pleaſure, who utterly denied that ſhe knew any thing of it, or was then aſhamed, at leaſt, to Own it; by which means her Life was preſerved. This Good-natur'd Merciful Biſhop, and Popiſh Prieſt, was not contented to Lop off Boughs and Branches, as he phras'd it at the Council-Board, but was for plucking up the Reformation by the Root, meaning Queen *Elizabeth*; and to do the *Spaniards* Juſtice, 'tis ſaid they interceded for her; perhaps it was only in Policy, that their Maſter might have Two Strings to his

his Bow, as it appeared by the sequel; for he Courted Queen *Elizabeth* after the Death of Queen *Mary*. 'Twas evident farther, how Queen *Mary* intended to keep her Word as to Religion, by her Match with *Spain*: No doubt she had a mind to put it out of her Power, and cast the Odium of Persecution off from her self. But we ought not to Reflect on her for Marrying one of her own Religion; since our Protestant Kings on this side the Reformation have had a good knack ever since of providing for the Security of the Protestant Religion by Popish Matches; for though King *James* the First did not actually Wed (he did not dare to have attempted it in *Scotland*) a Papist, yet he was more to blame in advising and pursuing One so hotly for his Son, than his Son who finished a Popish Match at last: This by the bye. The Rebellion of *Wyat* was an ill-tim'd Attempt begun too early (as another late One since); but had he let it alone a little longer, till Queen *Mary* shewed her self more fully in her proper Colours; when the Pope's Primacy came to be proposed and laboured to be Restored, and Cardinal
Pool

Pool. came over, it might have had another Effect, and proved a generous Effort for the Rescuing the Infant Reformation from the Jaws of Popish Tyranny: For the Pope had just Taught the People the way of being Absolved from their Allegiance; and they might infer if he could do it, or it were to be done for the sake of Religion, That they might Absolve themselves from their Allegiance for the good of Religion also. But when once a first Undertaking miscarries, through an ill-tim'd and rash Precipitation, a Second seldom or never comes to Maturity in the same Shape and Nature. Her Five Years Reign passed in a Hurry of Religion, Love, Persecution, Mariage, &c. with some Lunatick Intervals of Mercy. It is said her Reign was polluted with Blood of Martyrs, Unfortunate by frequent Insurrections, and Inglorious by the Loss of *Callis*. It is said also, she was a Lady of Good Nature and Merciful Disposition in her self; What then can we expect from the Reign of any Popish Prince, where the Barbarous Zeal, and Unhuman Authority of that Church, can so far Impose upon, and Over rule even a Merciful Prince, that Dr *Heylin*
calls

calls her's the greatest Persecution since *Dioclesian*'s time, and which raged most terribly. 'Tis truly and absolutely impossible for any thing of Honour, Virtue, or Good Nature, to have any place in a Sovereign under such a Sovereignty.

Queen Elizabeth.

IN the Reign of Queen *Elizabeth* we may obferve the difference in a method of Proteftant and Popifh Reformation, or Alteration of Religion: The Popifh under Queen *Mary* was begun and carried on by Imprifonments, Fire and Blood: The Proteftants by this Queen, with a true Chriftian Temper, by a gentle Remove, without any Blood, without Imprifoning any Perfon, and without inflicting almoft any Suffering or Penalty, till the Seditious Practices of the Popifh Party had provoked the Arm of Juftice; till the Pope had given away her Kingdom of *Ireland* as a *Heretick*; and *Parfons* and *Campian*, Two of his Emiffaries, had Depofed her at Home in their Doctrines. And after all, *Campian, Sherwin*, and *Briant*, did not fuffer as Popifh Priefts, but were Profecuted on the 25th of *Edward* the III^d for Plotting Deftruction of the Queen, and Ruin of the Kingdom; for Adhering to the Pope, the Queen's Enemy, and coming into *England* to Raife Forces

Forces against the State. And 'twas only for these Exorbitances of the Papists that new and strict Laws were Enacted against them in the following Parliaments, in the 23^d 27, 29, 35th Years of her Reign: Before that, there was only the Penalty of Twelvepence a *Sunday* for Absence from Church; and some other necessary provisions concerning the Supremacy, Administration of the Sacrament, and Form of Common-Prayer; which also were very tenderly put in Execution; and for above Twenty Years no Body suffered Death for Religion; nor till long after the Pope and King of *Spain* had conspired her Ruin, and *Gregory* the XIIIth held secret Consultations to Invade at once both *England* and *Ireland*; and longer after that Bloody Massacre of *Paris*; which was a design to Cut off the Protestants, as it was Termed; or at least to give them a deep Wound; and the terrible Slaughters of Protestants through all the Cities of *France*; and the War afterwards declared against the Protestants in the time of *Charles* the IXth; not to reflect on the *Chambres Ardentes* before against Protestants in *Henry* the II^d's time; and after the Attempt which the Duke of *Alva*, on the behalf of the Queen of *Scots*, and the just suspicions she might entertain on her account, who

was

was then accounted the great Patroneſs and only hopes of the Papiſts, and all the other Stratagems and viſible Deſigns of that Party. And the ſecond Execution of any Perſon was in her Twenty fifth Year, and upon a juſt neceſſity of Self-preſervation, upon the raſh and extravagant Proceedings of *Somervill* and Others. Beſides, when the Queen was informed even of theſe Severities (as they are call'd), tender ones in compariſon; ſhe grew offended with the Commiſſioners for Popiſh Cauſes, Reproved them for their Severity (although they declared and proteſted, they Queſtioned no Man for his Religion, but only for dangerous Attempts againſt her Majeſty and the State); and the Queen forbad them afterwards to uſe Tortures, as ſhe did the Judges other Puniſhments: And not long after that, when Seventy Prieſts were taken, and ſome of them Condemned, and the reſt in danger of the Law, ſhe only ſhipp'd them away out of *England*. A Merciful piece of Juſtice! So Merciful ſhe was, that it gave her Enemies ſuch Encouragement, as her Life was never ſafe; (as may appear by the Caſe of Dr *Parry*); till there was a neceſſity for an *Aſſociation* to provide for the Queen's ſafety, which was fiſſt Voluntary by a Number of her Subjects, the Earl of *Leicester* being foremost, thence after of all Ranks and Conditions bound mutually thereunto to each other by their Oaths and Subscriptions, *to Prosecute all those to the very Death*, that should Attempt any thing against the Queen, which the Year following was in a Parliamentary manner Enacted into a formal Law. Notwithstanding which, another dangerous Conspiracy of one *Savage*, set on foot by *Babington* and Others to take away her Life, as being Excommunicated, was discovered, and about Fourteen were justly Executed for Treason. Upon which last Treason hung the Fate of the Queen of *Scots*; the Justice whereof has been so much Controverted and Debated: Rules of Policy and Self-preservation must cashier all Principles of good Nature or Honour: Yet, however, Execution was not done upon her, till the *French* Ambassador and others, were again discovered to take off the Queen by way of prevention. And the Circumstances (suggested to the Queen at least) of the *Spanish* Navy being come to *Milford* Haven, the *Scots* into *England*, and that the Duke of *Guise* was Landed at *Sussex*, &c. may extenuate, if not excuse, the Severity of her Execution, with any

any but Papists; and the manner of doing it at last, shews it was Extorted from her upon inevitable Considerations, and Symptoms of a relucting necessity. Her often Countermanding it, demonstrates it was not an Act of her Inclination; and at last, perhaps, (as far as it appears) it was obtained of her by Surprise, and without her Authorising Hand to the finishing Stroke. If there were any thing in it of Barbarity, 'twas the denying her a Catholick Priest or Confessor, and the Manner of her Execution: Which yet is no more than Papists deny Protestants on all occasions; and I know not why we should not vouch the dying Honour of our Religion, as they do of theirs. But enough has been said of this Tragedy on all Hands; only it may be fit to Remark, That even the *French* Historians give a more favourable Account of it than our own, and particularly *Mezeray* is softer in his Expressions than *Baker*: The first says, " The In-
" discretion of her Friends was no less
" the Cause of her Misfortune, than the
" Wickedness of her Enemies; as the
" First sought with violent passion af-
" ter some plausible pretence to Ruin
" her, the Other furnished them with
" divers, by contriving every Hour some
" odd

"odd Design, and even Conspiracies
"against Queen *Elizabeth*; so that they
"made her Perish by their over-much
"Care and Endeavours to Save her.
The Later gives a slim, trimming Account, which was worse. Although 'tis true, the taking off the Queen of *Scots* did not break the Neck of the Popish Designs (for who can restrain the Malice of Jesuits? for Men must have some ingredient of Modesty to be convinc'd and silenc'd, and kept within the bounds of natural Virtue) yet it stopp'd their Hands for some time. And when afterwards they began again upon the Example and Encouragement of the Holy League in *France* (of which the Duke of *Guise* was Head, and in virtue of which they had taken off their own King, *Henry* the III^d, by the Hands of *James Clement* a Monk, though *Guise* himself was first Assassinated); and they had taken new heart upon the King of *Spain*'s Founding a Seminary of *English* at *Validolid*; and new Plots were contrived against the Queen: It put them somewhat out of the way, and they were at a loss where to find a Successor to the Crown for their purpose, when *Lopez* and *Patrick Cullen*, &c. were to have Killed the Queen: And they

they were forc'd to hunt after far-fetch'd Titles in the *Infanta* of *Spain*, and farther, for the Earl of *Essex* at Home (the Son of the Queen of *Scots* being a Protestant); and even at last they made but little of it: The Queen remained in Peace and Safety, and their Pretender *Essex*, was himself Executed for Treason. The Affairs of the Church were so prudently managed in her time with relation to Puritans as well as Papists, that she left it in a Condition to stand upon its own Legs, and maintain it self without Danger from Opposition; had it been preserv'd with the same continuance of Zeal and unshaken Fidelity by her Successors. As to her Civil Administration, the Heathen and *Mahumetans*, the *Persians* and Idolaters, the *Ethiopians* and *Muscovites*, name her with Reverence. And *Bossac* in one of his Letters to *Cecil* saith, *He that Excommunicated her, spoke of her with Honour.*

She chose her self a Wise Councel, and shewed her own Wisdom in being Advised by them. She had a hard Game to play with *Philip* of *Spain*, as well as her own Popish Subjects; yet she managed both softly and by degrees, and at last by Parliament fix'd and secured

secured the general Alteration in Religion, which she could never have done by her self. First-Fruits and Tenths were Restored to the Crown, and the Supremacy Confirmed to the Queen. She avoided Matrimony, whether upon any Consideration besides Prudence, I shall not enquire; by doing so, she preserv'd her self Head of the Church and State, and Mistress of her self as well as her Subjects; and Oblig'd and Silenc'd the Parliament by soft Answers of denial, when they Remonstrated to her for that purpose, and put an unanswerable Compliment upon them, by telling them, *She had placed her Affections upon her People in General.* But in matters of Religion she was no Courtier; after she had once declared her self a Protestant (though some pretend she Dissembled in her Sister's Days) she did not look back towards the Pope, did not shuffle in her Religion, but refused all Communication with him, and also generously declined all the Overtures of Advantage made by *Pius* the IVth. She equally despised his Threats and Temptations: Afterwards she readily and sincerely Assisted the Distressed Protestants, her Neighbours, on all Occasions. She provided every thing for the Strength and

and Honour of the *English* Nation, and saw it maintain'd in its True Glory both at Home and Abroad: Would not be wheadled, nor huff'd to betray it, but carry'd its Reputation farther Abroad than any of her Predecessors had, or Successors hitherto have done. She shew'd it the way to overcome even the Invincible Armada of *Spain*, which the *Spaniards* with all their Force and Fraud had provided to Invade us, and basely to Attack us by Surprize, when they were at the same time in a (Treacherous) Treaty of a Peace: And all this she did without oppressing her Subjects, well knowing (as she her self declared, when she remitted a Fourth Subsidy) that the Money was as sure in her Subjects Coffers as her Own. 'Tis said of her, Never Prince ruled with more Justice, and with her Justice mingled more of Mercy: She was term'd St. *Elizabeth* by some at *Venice*, for her Merciful returning home certain *Italians* which were taken Prisoners in the Invasion of 1588. And 'tis said, some told the Lord *Carleton*, being then Ambassador, That though they were Papists, yet they would never pray to any other Saint; a Compliment at that distance may be laid hold of at home, for an acknowledgment of a just Character.

But

But her Truest Character we may take from her own Behaviour, and from her own Mouth, because it seems to have nothing of Vanity in it: In her Speech to her last Parliament, 1601. she thus expresseth her self. " To be a King, " and to wear a Crown, is a thing " more Glorious to them that see it, " than it is Pleasant to them who bear it: " Though you may have had, and may " have many Mightier and Wiser Princes " sitting in this Seat, yet you never " had, nor shall have, Any that will " love you better. *Du Serres* says of the Reign of *Henry* the Fourth of *France*, her Contemporary: " It is a Sign of " a Happy Reign, when the Subject re- " joyceth to see their Prince: 'Tis probable he might mean it as well of Queen *Elizabeth*; Or we may apply it for him, as it was verified of her: For it was observ'd in her short Progresses, that People of all sorts would flock to see her? And not only that, (for I have known other Kings attended through Curiosity) but also what hearty Acclamations did they utter? As God save Queen *Elizabeth, &c.* and she would Reply, God bless you, my People all. Few Princes miscarry who have the Affections of the better part of their People: 'Twas for this

this Reason, I suppose, that the Mother of the Duke of *Guise*, her professed Enemy, said, " *Elizabeth* of *England* was the most Glorious and Happy Woman that ever swayed Scepter: And *Henry* the Fourth of *France*, in a Letter to Monsieur *de Rosny*, commends her with an implicit sort of Emulation. She had such a Character even with the *Turks* for Morality, and Natural Honour, That at her Instance he countenanced the *English* Trading there, and thence came, as is said, our *Turky* Company, and every one knows the Benefit of it to *England*. Also the Duke of *Russia*, for her sake, as is said, (who yet is so jealous of Strangers) gave Civil Reception to the *English*. In short, That Kingdom which she found in Troubles, and unsetled, she left Establish'd in True Religion, Peace and Plenty at Home, and Reputation Abroad.

JAMES

JAMES I.

I Dare not Encounter this King so rudely as some have done ('tis said upon good Experience): Nor would I be thought to offer Undecent Reflections at a King, who came Ushered into our Throne with such a Reputation for Wisdom of his own, and such Advantages of a Councel, left him fam'd for it. Yet in my own Opinion, and poor Observation, I can't for my Soul pay that mighty Veneration to his Character and Memory which the World would seem to demand. He seems to me to have stumbled at the Threshold in our Kingdom, and to have done a thing not very Honourable or Prudent. Who, after he had so poorly quitted the Resentments of his Mother's Death before, by a sort of Reflex Malice; yet in pious Memory of her Sufferings, and to revive the Reasons of them here, and as it were, to Countenance and Abet the *Norfolk* Family upon the same Foundations, forthwith calls the Lord *Thomas* and
Henry

Henry Howard, two Papists, to the Council, thereby intimating, as it were, hopes to the Papists, &c. which they were apt enough, no doubt, to conceive. Nor will his Pretended Apprehension of the Pope's Briefs to the Catholicks, excuse him: Tho Sir *Richard Baker*, (who was bribed by a Knighthood at his first coming over) represents him in the front, to have done it only upon Prudential Moves; that is, Fear: Thus he at first ish disobliged all Parties. And who knows, but this first Cast of Favour to them, and to the Earl of *Southampton*, whose Father, 'tis true, was a great Friend to *Mary* Queen of *Scots*, but a greater to Popery); and his partial, aukward Behaviour towards other Gentlemen, might be the Foundation of that complicated Treason by the Lord *Cobham*, Sir *Walter Rawleigh*, and others, Protestants and Papists, amongst whom were two Priests, and for which there was no other apparent Occasion, only that he provok'd all Parties, whilst he sought to win one, by Fawning; to shew something like good Inclinations to the See of *Rome*, as the Pope expected, though they well knew, he did not mean that either; whilst he received others coldly, for Reasons neither he nor they knew:

knew: So that they agreed, only in this, to lay him aside, who, as they concluded by his Behaviour, would answer the Expectations of neither. There was no necessity of adding Papists as Spies upon his Councels; he might in prudence been contented to have taken it at present, as left him, with the Addition only of his *Scotchmen* to the Number: And 'tis plain it gave no satisfaction to the Papists by the Powder-Plot which followed: His Next Step of Unaccountable Wisdom was dissolving the Parliament, for Reasons known to no body besides himself; 'tis said, because they did not comply with his Designs; but what those Designs were, do not appear Above-board. The Third Action of Moment, out of common Forms, was the sacrificing Sir *Walter Rawleigh* to the Importunities of *Gondomar* (for neither his Justice nor Mercy was to be relied on); that is, giving up the Interest of *England* to the *Spanish* Satisfaction. And his Conduct, with relation to *Spain*, is admirable throughout.

Queen *Elizabeth* had pretty well humbled that Potent Monarch; and, as Sir *Robert Cotton* observes, forced him in his after-Reign (that is, after his Unsuccessful

Government of England.

ıl Tricks with her) to that Ex-
, that he was driven to break all
vith those Princes that trusted
nd paid for One Year's Interest
wenty five thousand Millions of
: Hear Sir *Robert Cotton*, who
to the Person of King *James*,
refore we may assure our selves
y and gently: " So low and des-
: in Fortunes your Highness found
when you took this Crown;
from the abundant Goodness of
Peaceable Nature (this is the
of Banter, if Kings would see it)
vere pleas'd to begin your Hap-
eign with General Quiet, and
Spain first, which should have
ght in Noble Natures a more
ful Recompence than after fol-
l: For long it was not before
e was hearten'd to Rebel against
Highness; and flying, had a Pen-
it *Rome* paid him from the *Spa-*
\gent: His Son *Odonel Tyrconnel*,
others, your Chiefest Rebels, re-
ever since in Grace and Pay
the Arch-Duchess, at *Spain*'s De-
n. So soon as your Eldest Son
ly Memory, now with God, was
r Mariage, they began these Old
ns, by which before they had thri-
ven

"ven so well, *&c.* Thus Sir *R. C.* in that Stile.

And thus they led him on their Dance, whilst he Deserted (or, what was worse, so meanly Vindicated) the Interest of his Son-in-Law the Prince *Palatine :* He must take his Measures from *Gondomar*; and instead of assisting him with a Powerful Army, he is treating with this *Spanish* Agent, and must take his Advice, and Matters are to be made up with him, by a Match for his Son the Prince of *Wales*, with the *Infanta* of *Spain*; and then suffers himself to be imposed upon by Idle Representations, which this Ambassador carried on only in Disguise to serve his Master's Ends; whilst in the mean time the Poor *Palatine* is swallowed up by a Confederacy between the Emperor and King of *Spain*, and all this without calling a Parliament; that being, forsooth, an Affront to his Wisdom; then sends his Son to *Spain*, when he was told by Sir *John Digby, &c.* (who advised him not to suffer his Resolutions to be interrupted by that Overture) of the False Appearances and Insincerities of the *Spaniards*, which the Letters from the King of *Spain* to *Olivares*, and his Answer, would

have convinced any one of, be-
nſelf ; and after that, his making
y and ample Conceſſions in fa-
Popery during the Treaty. And
, Treating of any Popiſh Match,
great Arguments of Wiſdom, Fa-
are, or indeed of Religion : The
Navy muſt be neglected, on
intimated by *Gondomar*, that the
ng of it would breed ſuſpicion in
ng his Maſter ; and the Cautio-
owns muſt be rendred up, being
s of the Low-Countries, to ob-
Friend *Gondomar* too : His Peo-
England muſt be Check'd, Diſ-
, and Silenced, for oppoſing this
Match, with their Speeches,
ls, Wiſhes, and even Prayers ; ('tis
ondomar could Diſſolve Parliaments
The Proteſtant Intereſt on his
ccount in *Bohemia* ſlighted ; though
ſhop *Abbot* repreſented the Cir-
nces and Call of Religion to En-
him, beſides Honour : Though
nbaſſador *Cottington* inform'd how
rs went, and though every body,
himſelf, ſaw through the Deſigns
in, as well in the Complimenting
n the Match as Mediatorſhip, to
him Neuter, and hold him in Suſ-
: A though he himſelf ſaw it

turn

turn to a War of Religion, and would be the Overthrow of the Proteſtants or Evangelicks; and though the Emperor had proſcribed the Prince *Palatine*; yet King *James*'s Eyes would not be open'd, nor would be perſuaded to take the Alarm. Theſe are no great Maſter-ſtrokes of Policy, no more than of Conſcience or Honour: And to War at laſt, when all was loſt againſt his own avow'd Principles, was an Incomprehenſible Myſtery of Judgment and Wiſdom. Beſides theſe, of which he diſcharged himſelf thus learnedly, there was no Matter of Moment did or could Occur during his Reign, to exerciſe any Extraordinary Talent. As for the Governing his People, 'tis plain he had King-Craft, as his Friend Sir *Richard Baker* calls it, as is pretty Evident by his Parliamentary Speeches, and his Ways of getting Money. He could alſo Diſſemble, and ſometimes Huff, but 'twas only his own Subjects, and that with no good Grace neither.

He had Prieſt-Craft too, as *Heylin* obſerves, who tells us, " 'Twas his uſu-
" al Practice in the whole Courſe of his
" Government, to Balance one extreme
" by the other, Countenancing the Papiſts,

"pists against the *Puritans*, and the *Pu-*
"*ritans* sometimes against the Papists.
Thus he was Devout for the *Church
of England* at Home, and for Popery A-
broad; making Canons for their Conformity here, and submitting our Orders to Truckle to the Popish Match,
against all the Remonstrances of Parliament, Church, and People: What
could he expect from this Popish
Match, from any Popish Match, but
the Consequences all the World expected? That it would let in Popery
once more into Hopes of Success, at
least to gain Breath by a suspension
of the Laws against them: What could
be expected but that this must create
Jealousies and Misunderstandings between
him and his Subjects? And 'twas not
sending a Synod of Divines to *Dort*,
or having a Convocation at Home (of
which Dr. *Overal*, his Dean of *Paul's*,
has given a special Account for the
Edification of his Successor the present Dean) could likely settle the
Affairs of the Church in *Europe*, when
he at the same time was giving the
Pope a Lifting-hand, and rais'd his droop-
ing Head here so early after the Reformation; and when at the same time
the Protestants in *Germany*, *France*, and

I the

the Low-Countries, were groaning under a Perfecution. Which made *Du Pleſſis* complain, *Que Sa Majeſtie D'Angleterre trop arreſte à quelques petits, diſſenſions entre les Siens, n'evoit pas aſſez de ſoin de la guerifon de plus profondes playes qui ſont en l'Eglise* ; and which made the Houſe of Commons Petition and Remonſtrate in the Force of Fourteen Reaſons, and Ten Remedies, in the XIXth Year of his Reign; which had only this Effect, to make him fly to his old Refuge of Prerogative with a Huff: And that the Mariage of his Children, Peace and War, &c. were Matters of State and Government above their Conſiderations: And Speeching it backwards and forwards (which he took great Delight in) till his Son-in-Law was deſpoiled of his Ancient Patrimony, which he at laſt ingenuouſly confeſs'd was through his Default. Here's the Effect of Prerogative! Theſe Proceedings, I ſuppoſe, put Sir *Robert Cotton* upon Enquiry what the Kings of *England* had done in the like Caſes: And after great pains in the ſearch of Records, he informs us, "That the Kings of this " Nation, ever ſince the Conqueſt, ſo " ſoon as they were cool enough for " Councels, have uſually conſulted with
"their

"their Peers in the great Council, and
"Commons in Parliament, of Mariage,
"Peace, and War. He might have said before the Conquest also; for *Harold*, who had promised *William* Duke of *Normandy*, to take one of his Daughters to Wife, Answers, That he should be very injurious to his own Nobility, if he should without their Consent and Advice take a Stranger to Wife. If we look into our Neighbour Kingdoms, *Mezeray* will tell us, That the *French*, during the two first Races, and part of the third, had a Right to intermeddle and controul the Mariages of their Kings; and neither could the King make War without the Lords In earnest, I know not whether Kings in Reason ought to be permitted to Converse with Ambassadors on t'other side of Forms, upon their own Heads without a *Quorum* of their Councils: For Nations generally send the sharpest Men on such Errands, and sometimes Kings are not a Match in Politicks for them, as it plainly appeared by this Story this King was not for *Gondomar*, who outwitted him, who pretended to be the wisest. But King *James* came over to us, Tinctur'd with his *Scotch* Notions of Monarchical and Sovereign

Abſolute Power, without vouchſafing ever after to conſider the *Engliſh* Conſtitution; and he lets us ſee what Opinion he had of Parliaments in his Βασιλικὸν Δῶρόν, wherein he "Adviſes his "Son to hold no Parliaments but for Ne- "ceſſity of new Laws, which would be "but ſeldom: Nor, it ſeems, for the State, Matters of War, Mariage, *&c.* No, not for raiſing Money neither, ſo long as he could get it by Privy-Seals and Benevolences. Beſides, after all, he did not come hither without ſome Prejudices to the *Engliſh* People, though he had none to the Crown of *England.* Thus there may ſeem to be ſome inconveniences in a Learn'd Crown'd Head: This King thought himſelf too Wiſe, and too Knowing; He was above Advice or Inſtruction, becauſe, as he thought, he was capable of giving it: He was too wiſe in himſelf to be taught by others, and yet not wiſe enough always to follow thoſe Rules of Wiſdom which he had given; As is evident by the Obſervation of his Theory and Practice; and by his inconſiſtent Directions to his Sons, *Henry* and *Charles.* He was a little too much addicted to the Pedantry of a Scholar, and affected with Polemical Controverſies in Words, which he dreaded in Action :

on: Was more for determining Quarrels by the Pen, than the Sword: And perhaps might have made a better Bishop than a King; a better Father of a Family, than Country; as being better seen in the Oeconomicks, than Political Government of a Nation.

CHARLES I.

Montaign, (whom I confess I delight to bring in as often as I can, though I know the Philosophers are angry with him, for I do not pretend to be a better Politician, or any thing else than he was; The Grave have Gravity in them, but I know not what besides,) says, "That about a Month since, he read over two *Scotch* Authors, of which he who stands for the People, makes Kings to be in a worse condition than a Carter; and he who writes for Monarchy places him some Degrees above God Almighty in Power and Sovereignty: I'm sorry there is no Medium; and I know no Necessity for Either. Who those two *Scotch* Authors were, ev'ry one knows: King *James* complain'd of one of them, and advanc'd t'other, as it always happens to them who stretch for Kings. Such have been the Notions of Government in both Extremes, and both were unhappily experimented in this Reign. This King, flush'd I doubt

with such Authors as the last, and perhaps withal observing what was done in *France* under *Lewis* the XIth, who boasted that he had *mis le Royaum hors du Page*, " as he calls it; and who, as *Mezeray*
" observes, had even Government with-
" out Council, and most commonly with-
" out Justice and Reason: Who thought
" it the finest Policy to go out of that
" great and beaten Road of his Prede-
" cessors, to change ev'ry thing, were it
" from better to worse, that he might
" be fear'd: His Judgment which was
" very clear, but too subtle and refin'd
" (as was that of King *James*) was the
" greatest Enemy to his own and his
" Kingdom's quiet, having, as it seems,
" taken pleasure in putting things into dis-
" order, and throwing the most Obedi-
" ent into Rebellion: Who rather lov'd
" to follow the bent of his own irre-
" gular fancies, than the wise Laws of
" the Land; and made his Grandeur
" consist in the Oppression of his Peo-
ple, &c. And also in the Reign of *Henry* the IVth, who gave the last stroke to Parliamentary Formalities, and Huff'd the People into a new Law, that from thenceforth the King's Edicts should be ratified on sight, without those formal triflings of Dispute, by Virtue of Living

and Ruling always with his Sword in his Hand, might conceive some such great Hopes. These Reflections might perhaps inspire King *Charles* with the *French* Ayre of Grandeur; but a People is sometimes quick-sighted too: And hence on a sudden grew an impertinent (as it then seem'd) Jealousy between King and People: One pretending to too much after one Author, and t'other yielding too little by the other: Whilst the former might be Nibbling at Arbitrary Power in an Extended Prerogative, and the latter enlarging their Liberties somewhat beyond a modest Bound; and there were Courtiers in those Days also, such as *Philip de Comines* observ'd, in Court Language to Complement a King, call'd it Rebellion to mention a Parliament; and *Lewis* also was a superstitious Friend to the Church, whilst he was assaulting and oppress'd the State. In these and such like Circumstances of Notional Government, in such State of picqueering Misunderstanding, King *James* left his Crown to King *Charles*, and in a War for Recovery of the *Palatinate* without any Money, and in a fair way of Quarrel at Home, as well as Abroad. Besides, the People had it in their Memories and Consideration, his Complaisant

Be-

Behaviour in *Spain*, his Letter to, and Tampering with the Pope in Order to that Match, which rais'd new Jealousies on Account of Religion; and his Compleating himself the Match with *France* with as Frank Articles for Popery, as had before been offer'd to *Spain* in Conjunction with his Father, confirm'd them in them.

These Reasons and Considerations took possession justly enough in the Minds of Men, which made them ever after stand upon their guard: And setting aside all those Scurrilous Authors on the One hand, who have pretended to give us a Narrative of his Actions; and also those Fulsome Ones, on the Other; all those who would Depress or Advance his Character with Art; certainly a great many Actions of his Administration are not to be justified in a Court of Honour or Wisdom: Such as Dissolving the First Parliament meerly in Complaisance to the Duke of *Buckingham*: A King must necessarily Disoblige and Affront the Community, when he Espouseth the Interest of a Single Person against the Publick; and it shews a Weakness to put one Man (no better than the rest) in the Scales in competition with Mankind, as
it

it were: But especially a King ought to be sure the Subject-matter of such Protection and Preference is good and justifiable, otherwise he commits a double Error. It will be thought Ill-natur'd to Argue against Favourites; but I must Argue against the Argument for them: It is a very odd Inference, That because our Saviour had his Favourite-Disciple, therefore Kings must have their Favourites: I suppose No body will pretend there is any parity of Reason.

To return therefore to the Duke of *Buckingham*, who, without Dispute, had betrayed the Vantguard, &c. to the *French*, after the King and he knew both that they were to be employed against the *Rochellers*; this was in it self a great Abuse to the Honour of the *English* Nation, and a manifest Injustice and Injury to the Protestant Religion. And 'twas from this King's Reign that the *French* began to Date their Strength at Sea. This only Action bred such ill Blood, and created so great a Misunderstanding at first between the King and his Subjects, as stuck to the Duke of *Buckingham* till his Death, whom *Felton* kill'd; and, I doubt, till the King's too.

His

His next Proceeding was Extraordinary, when he had thus Dissolv'd the First Parliament: To Levy Money by Privy Seals, which had so ill a favour in his Father's Time, and then to call a Parliament presently on the neck of that Miscarriage, and to side with the D. of B. against the E. of B. and the denying the latter his Writ to Parliament; this lookt inconsiderate, and a little mean; and the interposing so much on behalf of the former, even with passion as well as partiality, had but an ill grace. I pass by the Business of the Earl of *Arundel*, which also could not but breed ill Blood in the House of Peers. By the King's Obstinacy in these Affairs (though I do not pretend to justify the House of Commons in theirs), instead of preserving one Friend, in the mean time he sacrifices all the rest to his Humour: For the King of *Denmark*, who (at his Instance chiefly) had taken up Arms in his Quarrel, was beaten, and reduced to great Distress, for want of Succors from *England*, which the King had thus disabled himself to supply according to his Promise. That Necessity put him again upon Indirect Courses for Raising of Money by Commissions of Loan, and seising all Duties

of

of Customs, Privy-Seals, Benevolences, &c. as if he would shew he design'd, if he had prevail'd, to live on himself without a Parliament. But the Imprisoning the Gentlemen for refusing the Loan, and the Suspending and Disgracing Archbishop *Abbot* for refusing to License *Sibthorp*'s Book, were Strains of Arbitrary Power, which exposed Religion as well as Law into a Jest; and seem to profane the Sacred Title of a King, as well as that of an Archbishop; as appears especially in that Archbishop's Narrative and Dialogue, with the Passages therein express'd, if it be true, which exposes that whole Transaction as a plain Rhodomontade and Defiance to all Rules of Justice and Reason. I will take notice only of the Observation of the Archbishop upon the Fourth Objection to *Sibthorp*'s Sermon, by which you may guess at the rest: To the Fourth; "Let the "Largeness of those words be well consi- "der'd, says the Archbishop; yea all "Antiquity to be absolutely for Abso- "lute Obedience to Princes in all Civil "or Temporal things, for such Cases as "*Naboth*'s Vineyard may fall within this; "and if I had allow'd this for Doctrine, "I had been justly beaten with my own "Rod: If the King the next day had
 "com-

"commanded me to send him all the
"Money and Goods I had, I must, by
"my own Rule, have obey'd him: And
"if he had commanded the like to all
"the Clergy of *England*, by *Sibthorp*'s
"Proposition, and the Archbishop of *Can-*
"*terbury*'s allowing of the same, they
"must have sent in all, and left their
"Wives and Children in a Miserable
"Case; yea the Words extend so far,
"and are so absolutely deliver'd, that by
"this Divinity, If the King should send
"to the City of *London*, and the Inha-
"bitants thereof, commanding them to
"give unto him all the Wealth they
"have, they were bound to do it: There
"is a *Meum & Tuum* in Christian Com-
"monwealths; and according to Laws
"and Customs Princes may dispose of it.
"That Saying being true, *Ad Reges Po-*
"*testas omnium pertinet, ad singulos proprie-*
"*tas*. This was the Sense of the Archbishop on this Matter; and yet the King
espoused the Fancies of a *Sibthorp* against
him, who was not so much as a Batchel-
lour of Arts, only for the merit of his
Flattering Divinity: And in truth the
whole Proceeding is apt to turn one's
Stomach; besides, that the King in Ex-
posing the Dignity of a Person of such a
Figure in the Church, did also make
bold

bold with his own Character at second hand, who stood but one Remove Higher. And what was it but to intimate to the Lay-Gentlemen, that neither of them were so sacred or inviolable as was pretended: And, by the by, 'tis not safe to make too Light of a Spiritual Person, they can't be held too sacred on this side of Infallibility: But how like a Prophet did the Archbishop talk? How did he Reason like a Statesman concerning the King and Duke of *Buckingham*? How did the Event but too well justify the Predictions? What could the King expect from his Next Parliament, which he was in a manner forc'd to Call, after the Imprisonment of so many Gentlemen, and the Poor-spirited Way of Releasing them, which lookt almost as bad as the Imprisoning them? What could he say after that Unfortunate Action in the *Isle of Rhee*? 'Twould make one sick to reflect on Sir *Robert Cotton*'s Speech and Advice, in comparison with the Giddy Peevish Measures taken at Court. What Event that Parliament was like to have, may be seen, together with the Talent of these two Kings, the Father and Son's King-Craft, in the Jesuits Letter, in the Speeches within Doors and without, and in the Petitions, Debates and Remonstrances, stances, after that the King had brought himself and his Honour in Jealousy with the People, and the People understood the Circumstances of his Administration, and Pressures of his Affairs. But to shew there were some Dispositions to Agreement, the King's granting the Petition of Right had almost reconciled and soften'd all these Discontents and Misunderstandings; till the Old Bone was thrown in again, and the Business, that unhappy Business of the Duke of *Buckingham*, resumed, which caused Ill-natur'd Reflections, and in which, perhaps, all Parties were too stiff: Hence the Old Game was plaid over again. This set up the Dispute of Tunnage and Poundage; this Prorogued the Parliament, and after many Exorbitant Bickerings about Religion, and Levying this Duty, or Branch of the Revenue, the Blood was put into such a ferment, that although the Duke of *Buckingham* was gone, the Parliament was dissolved in a heat. It is pretty hard to find an Impartial Comment on the Transactions of these Times: By what appears, no doubt some Members of the House of Commons had behaved themselves insolently enough; but to do Justice on the other hand, there was some provocation on the King's Part,

not

not only before, but after the Death of the Duke of *Buckingham*. The preferring *Montague* to a Bishoprick for his *Appello Cæsarem*, and *Manwaring* to another Good Benefice, with a Dispensation, in contradiction to the Parliament, who had Censured and perpetually disabled him for the future to Ecclesiastical Preferment in the Church of *England*; and taking *Laud* into so peculiar favour, as in pious Memory of the Duke of *Buckingham* (for otherwise he had been obnoxious to Censure justly); and making *Weston* Treasurer, who died a Papist; and *Windebank* afterwards Secretary of State: Besides these Odd Promotions, the Malicious and hard Prosecution of the Merchants, even to Ruin, for not paying the Customs; and the little Overtures which were discover'd for breaking Parliaments for the future, and to set up Something in Imitation of the Assembly *des Notables*, (for he always collogued with the Lords) to introduce what should be very like Arbitrary Power; These were all things of ill digestion, and did not look like Touches of a Complexion with a Limited Monarchy. I take no notice of the Affairs in *Scotland*, nor of some Intervening Transactions at Home, which are Mysterious, and prov'd Unfortunate, though they might

might bear a candid Conſtruction with ſome. The Buſineſs of Ship-Money was the Invention of his Attorney-General *Noy*; and the Project was backt with the Opinion of all the Judges *obiter*, and confirm'd by the Judgment of Ten of them on mature Deliberation: But how unhappily ſoever that Affair was reſented, and ſucceeded at laſt, this at leaſt muſt be ſaid in vindication of the King, That he did apply the Money to the true Uſe; did equip a Gallant Fleet with it, whereupon our Trade was not only made ſecure by ſcowring the Seas of Pyrates, but in aſſerting the Honour of the *Engliſh* Nation; ſaved *Flanders* from being ſwallowed up between the *French* and *Dutch*; reſcued the Fiſhery from the Incroachment of the latter by ſeizing or diſperſing their Buſſes, which were fiſhing on our Coaſts, and made them petition humbly, for what they before by force of *Grotius*, and by force of Arms, arrogantly aſſerted, and claim'd as a Right; and thus maintain'd the Dominion of the Seas, and advanc'd the Reputation of the Kingdom Abroad.

But we will now come again to the Church, which firſt and laſt diſorder'd the Scene of Affairs in the State: Here we see the Misfortune of a Popish Match, which renders all Things and Persons suspected, and gives a latitude for Enemies to work by Mines, who could not have hurt Us by Batteries. This makes an Archbishop, who was guilty only of Pride and Rashness, suspected for Popery also: Whilst Cardinal *Richlieu* behind the Curtain, and Nuntio's, Priests and Jesuits in Masquerade, blow up the Coals, till they had kindled the Nation into a War; and not only that, but their Priests personally engage in it, for fear it should not effectually be carried on, unless they were in it on both Sides. That these things are true, is past all doubt; and as to the last, it appears by *Mentet Hist. de Troubles de Grand Britain*, who must be admitted to be a Faithful Author on this Account.

And here we are launch'd into a troubled Sea; here I desire to draw the Curtain; for all the rest of this Unfortunate King's Life is too Troubled and Stormy for Calm Remarks of Policy. His Consideration came too late, I believe, even from the first want of it; the first foundations of Jealousy were so strong, that all the other subsequent Debates could signify nothing towards Satisfaction; all the consequential Meetings and Parliaments

ments, were Tumults rather than Counsels, after the *Scotch* Air of Sedition blew this way; the first false Measures are seldom or never to be retriev'd. All this King's subsequent Actions could never absolutely undeceive his People; they must still believe him Popishly affected, though they were almost convinc'd he was not a Papist. 'Tis impossible to dispossess an enraged Multitude, and difficult to satisfy generous Minds under prepossessions and prejudices of Opinion. The Wounds were too deep for a gentle Cure. I presume not to Arraign or Justify his Conduct: He seems to have been a better Man than King; and a better Churchman than he was believed to be: 'Tis evident, beyond possibility of doubt, that he was charged falsly with being a Papist. But when a Man has brought himself to the circumstances of Trimming between two Extremes, he is in danger of being Crush'd by Both. And that had been King *James*'s Fate, no doubt, had he been link'd to a Papist as well as his Son; whereas had King *Charles* Married one of the same Persuasion, neither his own Trimming, nor his Father's would have hurt him; but having Married a Papist, his Father's Insincerity and Priest-craft Ruined the Son, without descending upon him. For Popish Priests, so long as we Harbour them, will sting one way or other. *Henry* the III^d and IVth of *France*, fell by the Hands of a couple of Priests, upon another sort of suspicion; but Ours at second hand from Priests, who were not contented only to Kill him, unless they Destroyed the Constitution also. Hard Circumstances of this poor King! to be pursued by the Fanatick Party as giving too great Countenance to Papists, and by the Papists for not giving them enough, and not coming up to answer their Expectations. This I take to be the Case, and this the true Consequence of the Popish Match; and Popery was at the bottom: For though it be said the Puritans had a Design to throw him out of the Saddle, right or wrong, and that nothing of Concessions should ever satisfy them; (and this, perhaps, may be true of some very sower Zealots, and extravagant Pretenders); yet 'tis improbable, and what they could never have hoped for; and the greater part of the Presbyterians were drawn in by Surprise, who did not foresee the end, and withdrew afterwards, when, 'tis true, 'twas too late. But after all, the design was carried on in other Nations

tions besides our own, and by other Councels beyond ours: And Popish Priests had not only their Heads but Hands also in the Business, not only in Peace but War likewise; as you may read in *Mentet*; who would not lie in that Affair; 'tis a pretty scarce Book, and therefore I will give you his Words; he says, speaking of the Battel of *Edge-Hill*, *Ce que surprit le plus tout le Monde ce fut qu' on trouva quelques Prestres parmi les Morts du Costé des Estates: Car Encore que Dans leurs Manifestes ils appellassent l' Armeé du Roy l' Armeé des Papistes pour le rendre Odieux au Peuple, ils avoient neamoins deux Compagnies de Wallons & d'autres Catholiques dans leur Armeé, Outre qu'ils avoient rien oublié pour tascher d' engager en leur Partie le Chevalier* Arthur Afton, *Colonel Catholique de grand Reputation*. And he says before, That the King published an Edict at *Stonely* (afore that) wherein he tells them, He did not mean that any Papist should come to serve in his Army, that he might not give Discontent or Jealousy to his Protestant Subjects; but then 'twas too late for such like Overtures of Honour or Professions of Sincerity. But to go on with *Mentet*; *Il est vray que le Roy avoit aussi son ert dans son Armeé quelques Officiers Catholiques, Homes de*

K 3 *grand*

grand suffisance & les bien intentionées pour le bien de l' Estat, ainsi les appella't 'il, dans la declaration qu' il' fit publier apres le Battail, à quoy les Estates n' oublierent pas de repondre par autant des Contredits. Il temoigne qu' encore que les Estates eussent sans Comparison plus grand Nombre des Catholiques, que luy dans leur Armeé, & qu' ils eussent tasché, par toutes sortes de moyens de gaigner tous ceux du Royaume leur ayant fait promettre sous main que moyennant qu' ils voulussent prendre partie avec eux. On abrogeroit toutes les Ordinances faites à leur prejudice: Il ne pouvoit toute fois se resoudre d' appeller les Catholiques à son secours n'y de revoquer son Edit por le quel il leur avoit fait des defenses de s'y presenter: Il asseure de plus tous les bons sujets que bien qu' il eust regard aux personnes des Catholiques qui l' avoient secouru dans sa Necessité & qu' il eust bonne Memoire de leur Services, il ne feroit pourtant jamais rien en faveur de leur Religion, &c. All this came too late for our purpose; yet if this, and his Manifesto at the beginning of the *English* and *Scotch* Presbytery; if his Letters to the Queen taken at *Naseby*, wherein he protests to differ in nothing from her but Religion; if his other Conferences with the Marquess of *Worcester*, *cefter*, &c. and his Εἰκὼν Βασιλική, and his Dying Speech will not satisfy Men, that he was no Papift; they feem to be as Cruel to his Memory as they were to his Perfon: Though after all, his Articles of Mariage were too Frank for a Church-of-*England*-Man, who was not in Love at the fame time: And the *Spanifh* Match, if either, might probably, have had fomewhat a better Succefs, for this Reafon only, That the King of *Spain* was going down the wind, whereas the *French* King was advancing; and I muft repeat it, the Obfervation of what his Brother of *France*, *Lewis* the XIIIth, was doing but juft on t'other fide of the Water, increas'd our Jealoufies on this, and gave an incurable Wound to the King's Reputation. This made the People, with fome colour of Reafon, by way of prevention, endeavour to wreft the Sword out of the King's Hands, and attempt to get the Militia into their own; upon this pretence the Parliament were forward to put a falfe Conftruction upon his Raifing of Forces, and turn'd it to a Levying of War on the People, in order (as they call'd it) to fubvert the Laws, and introduce an Arbitrary Tyrannical Government; whereas we have the King's Word

Word for it, *That he took up Arms only to Defend the Fundamental Laws of the Kingdom*; and in his Dying-Speech he tells the World, *He did never intend to incroach upon the Privileges of the People, and that he desired their Liberty and Freedom as much as any body whatsoever; and that he died a Martyr of the People*, meaning, I suppose, for them. And after all, these Proceedings are so unaccountable, that they can't be reconciled to any Rules of Political Observation; there seems to be somewhat of Fate in them, which will not be confined to our little narrow ways of Reasoning, nor to the more enlarged deep Politicks of Statesmen. The Event exceeded the Scheme laid by *Richlieu*, and the Expectations of his Successor *Mazarine*; who at first, being surpriz'd, did prosecute the King's Death with some Resentment; though after (like a true Politician) he kept Correspondence with *Cromwell*. It seems their design was only to Embroil *England*, whilst *France* carried on its Designs elsewhere; not to Establish any setled Power, not a Commonwealth certainly: Their Business was but to Embarass our Councels, that they might be at liberty to follow theirs without Interruption. Not to Establish any Religion, not even Popery;

ry; for even Religion was not their Business, if it could have procured Peace and Prosperity to the Kingdom: But only to Counterpoise the two Extremes of Popery and Fanaticism (after the manner of King *James*) for a while, and to set the Fanaticks themselves by the Ears at last. Thus their Correspondents, their Agents, and their Money, was employed on all Hands to confound us in *England*, as well as the Jesuits had done all *Europe* by their Intriegues before, and we must fatally run into their Noose.

But there yet farther seems to be some extraordinary Hand in the Turn of these Affairs, above the Common Councels or Actions of Man, though not to be adjusted to Human Measures of Comprehension. Who knows what to say to the Prophecy of *Nostredamus*, (setting aside the *Scotch* Predictions, and those nearer home) *viz.* *The Senate of* London *shall put their King to Death?* 'Tis so very peculiar, though Printed almost an Hundred Years before, that it must intimate something, and even this or nothing. This, and those which *Mezeray* reports to have preceded the Death of *Henry* the IVth of *France*, particularly that Ticket which a Priest found upon an Altar at *Montargis*, giving notice that

the

the King would be Assassinated; his Horoscopes which determined the Year of his Life, and even the Queen's own Dream that the King was Stabbing with a Knife, (to pass by all others relating to this and other Occasions) must import this at least, to use *Mezeray*'s own Words (who, I believe, was no more Superstitious this way than my self) *That there is a Sovereign Power which Disposes of Futurity, since it so certainly Knows and Foretels it.* But this Subject is not my Part. Nevertheless, in truth, there appears to have been some extraordinary Conjunctions of the Planets, or something more. Extraordinary which gave that extravagant Turn to Powers here below, not only in *Europe*, but other remote parts of the World, and put sublunary Motions in such a Ferment about these Times, as was evident in the Kingdoms of *England*, *Scotland*, and *Ireland*, *Spain*, *Germany*, *France*, *Portugal*, and *Naples*, and the Hurly-burlies and Revolutions there, and in several other Parts; but also between the *Tartars* and *Chineses*, and in the Empire of the Great *Mogul*, between *Cha-gehan* and his Four Sons, especially *Aureng-zeb*; the Story whereof is Famous, and you may Read it at large in *Tavernier*: Which *Aureng-zeb* Sir *William Temple* calls a Fanatick, and compares

to

to *Cromwell*; as if all such strains of Empire were Enthusiastical, like that of the Great *Turk*. But to return to take my leave of King *Charles*; Morally speaking, I think the Queen was the Chief Occasion of all those Misfortunes which attended Him and the Nation, for there is no reason the Welfare of a Kingdom should hang at a King's Codpiece. The King's Marrying a Papist gave the suspicion of Popery, and the suspicion brought in Popery in Earnest.

CHARLES

CHARLES II.

AS to the first Twelve Years of the Nominal Reign of this King, 'twas such a Farce of Policy and Government, that it Libels the Chronicle; and I believe he had been sooner in his Throne, if he had never made a Step to help himself, by the Disturbance of those who usurp'd his Place. I wish for his Honour in the beginning, he had not intermedled with the Action of *Montross* during the Treaty with the *Scots*; it reflected some Aspersion upon his Sincerity, and he only sacrificed one Friend's Life, and the Reputation of others, and thereby prejudiced his own Interest for the present. But I know that Business hath also another Face, and therefore I pass by that, and some other Occurrences, to proceed to his own Administration after he was Crowned in *England*: Which I shall touch but very slightly neither, as slightly as he did the Interests of the Nation; the History of these Times being fresh in every one's Memory, I am very much at a loss

(con-

(considering the different Opinions of him, and his Inconsistency with himself) with what Character to introduce this King to his Government. If he was a Protestant when he came over to Us, as all his fine Declarations, &c. import, surely the Devil ow'd Us a shame (pardon the Expression) that we should blunder on a Popish Match again at first dash: Here was a loose given to the Papist and Fanatick to play their Old Game over again, and he put himself under a necessity of Suspition with his People once more: For let a Prince make what Gracious Speeches he pleases, his Actions will be always more significant, and speak plainer than his Declarations: Hence this Dilemma became entailed; either he doth answer the Expectations of the Papists or not: If he doth, and gives them any Assurances, &c. his own People are upon his Skirts: If not, then he is attack'd by the Indefatigable Plots and Attempts of the Jesuits, and that Party.

In the mean time, in what a blessed Condition of Settlement is a Nation? It can never be at quiet. I shall not pretend to dive into the Mysteries of one Plot or t'other, let them stand on their own Bottom in the validity of the Records.

cords. No doubt there always hath been a Popish Plot of one sort or other (more or less, as our Kings have given them a helping hand) ever since the Reformation; and, I believe, ever will be, so long at least as our Kings manage Affairs as they did for the Four last Reigns: And for ought I know too there may have been a Fanatick Plot ever since *Calvin*'s time, and will continue as long as Kingly Government and Church-Hierarchy are in fashion. Neither shall I trouble my self to enquire which Plot was the Agressor, which Plaintiff, which Defendant; which the Original, and which the Counter-plot: But between them both, this King had reduced himself to a pretty Condition of Trouble, if any thing could be so to him, by his Trimming, (a Quality which was scouted in the Subject): For in the Popish Plot he was to be taken off, for not being a Papist, or at least for not coming up to their Expectations of him; and by the Fanatick Plot he was to be Blunderbuss'd and destroy'd for being a Papist, and favouring their Designs too much: But to determine the precedence of these Plots: I think the Popish Plot first appeared upon the Stage against him, and it is thought, attended him at his *Exit*, though he died of their own Persuasion: I mean

I mean the Popish was the first Plot of Quality; for I take no notice of such little Things, as the Extravagant Matter of *Venner*, or that in the *North*, which was but a Fag-end of that in *Ireland*, and scarce then setled; nor of any thing of that nature which happen'd before the Year 1670. I do not find any Plot of Consequence till after the Acts of Parliament against Dissenters; not taking notice of the *Act of Uniformity*; or that against Quakers; but not till after that against Dissenting Preachers in Corporations, that against Conventicles, which came after the Declaration for Liberty of Conscience, and, as far as I can see, without any great provocation; which Acts, as they themselves speak, were grounded chiefly on Surmise and Suspition. Thus was he fain to shuffle on, sometimes in the form of Persecution against Dissenters, sometimes in that of Toleration and Indulgence to them and their Tender Consciences; so that Religion grew a meer State-Weather-Cock, as Circumstances happen'd, and turn'd as Court-Cabals mov'd, now one way, now another. Whereas, if he had come over a True Church-of-*England* Man, as he pretended to profess himself; he might have reduced the Church easily enough to some degree of Unifor-

Uniformity, and modell'd the Civil Government, and Ecclesiastical State, to a good Temper, having the Military Power in his own hands by the Militia Acts. But I suppose that was not his Business. And he discover'd the same Unsteadiness in Civil Matters; shifting Ministers and Officers, Proroguing and Dissolving Parliaments without apparent Reasons; and, 'tis said, for very bad Ones sometimes, and at very Evil Instances also. 'Twas the same thing in Military Affairs; Raising Armies to take the Air, and then Disbanding them abruptly; sometimes with the *French* against the *Dutch*, and then with the *Dutch* against the *French*; so Unconstant and Variable in his Councels and Himself: In truth he did not love to be tied to any thing, not even to a Mistress; and as very fond as he pretended to be of Parliaments once, he found Expedients, if they did not present themselves, to shake hands with them (after that long one that he was almost married to) very lightly shook them off as Uneasy Monitors; and, I believe, would have liked a Triennial Wife much better than a Triennial Parliament: And 'tis almost pity, that his first Choice was made by him (or rather for him) that he had not had an Opportunity of Wedding once more,

more, to have tried if he or they could have made a more improper Choice. In short, his Court and his Camp were a Jest, I had almost said his Church too; So far on Civil Supposition that he was a Protestant: But Sir *William Temple*, in his *Memoires*, scurvily intimates, That he was a Papist, and had a Design of setting up the same Religion and Government here, as that in *France*; and that he had his Pentionary Ministers and Cabals for that purpose, &c. I'm sorry if this was the only thing he was serious in! If this be true, he failed in his Designs, and shew'd himself no more a good Politician, than a good King: For whereas (as 'tis said) he might have given Laws to his Neighbours, by a well-grounded Peace or War; he was imposed upon to take them from them; and was nothing at Home, as *Gourvile*, (who is said to be the soundest *French*-Head) observed, reflecting on him; *Qu'un Roy d' Angleterre qui veut estre l' homme de son peuple, est le plus Grand Roy du Monde; mais s'il veut estre quelque chose d'advantage, par Dieu, il n'est plus rien.* 'Twas boldly expostulated by Sir *William Temple*, and well answered by the King; *Et je veux estre l' Homme de mon peuple*, if he could have held to it, as well as said it: But there was something else behind, or within the Curtain: However this Mat-ter

ter was, it seems, the King had managed his Affairs so, that he had no more Reputation for his Sincerity Abroad, than he had at Home: The States of *Holland*, and the Prince of *Orange* himself, had his Ministers and him in suspition, and his own Faction or Cabal divided against him, as knowing he was not to be depended upon; and the Parliament it self also had him in Jealousy: What a Figure is such a King like to make, when he and his Parliament encounter one another with Contradiction and Tricks! And when his taking Liberty of Conscience gave more Offence, than his giving of it! He was, besides, thought somewhat too much addicted to Pleasures, to apply himself to any thing serious: Not that, I think, those Reliefs are to be disallow'd: No man would be a King, if he were not to be allowed to soften his Cares with Diversions, and to sweeten them with Advantages of Delights; but he ought not, certainly, to suffer them to interfere with the Publick Consultations, and Clash with the Considerations of the Welfare of his People: And this is said to be his fault. He was so much given up to Softness, that he abhorr'd Application and Business; but, perhaps, he had other Reasons, besides, against too much Intenseness of Thought and Reflection:

flection: He might have the Success of the *English* Interest, as then Constituted, no more in his Wishes, than his Thoughts; Sir *William Temple* hath an Unhappy Observation this way, which I doubt applied it self; *viz.* "I have observed "from all that I have seen, or heard, "or read in Story, That nothing is so "fallacious, as to Reason upon the "Councels or Conduct of Princes or "States, from what one conceives to "be the true Interest of their Coun- "tries; for there is in all Places an In- "terest of those that Govern, and Ano- "ther of those that are Governed: (Hard "Saying!) And therefore I could never "find a better way of judging the Resolu- "tions of a State, than by the Personal "Temper, Understanding, or Passions, or "Humours of the Princes, or Chief "Ministers that were for that time at "the head of Affairs. 'Tis true, he gives the King a very handsome Character afterwards; but 'tis such a one, that seems to be restrained to his Private and Natural, not his Publick or Politick Capacity; as if a very fine Gentleman were spoiled, to make a very Indifferent King: And certainly he had more Vertues one way than t'other. I do not think he was Covetous; but I can't commend his Liberality, in being Generous at the Expence

pence of others, and free of his Subjects Purses: Thus he had rather be at the charges of a Pentionary Parliament, than at the pains of treating Fairly and Above-board. I shall not engage with the Secrets of this Court, they are too much a Mystery for me to dive into: Only I shall infer this Political Observation, That the Affairs of this Nation have never gone well, when the Councels of Parliament have been very much an Intrigue: They ought to be no more reserv'd, than too much expos'd: But there is One thing the People always will expect to be made privy to, that is, the Application of Money given; for if it come from them, they will always, and with Reason, know the Occasion; and will not endure to see it misapplied: Especially as the Circumstances of the Revenue then stood, his Income was certainly known, though I do not think the state of it was alter'd for the better in all Respects: The King had lost some Privileges in parting with those Commanding-Tenures; and though his Revenues might be thought ascertain'd, yet if it were not precarious, 'twas somewhat odious, and to be improv'd by the Debaucheries and Vices of his People. Hence, and by the Example of the Court, the Nation began to be Lewd, Head-

Headſtrong and Diſſolute: Laws of Temperance, Frugality, and Good Manners, were let looſe, and the Execution of them became in a little time a Jeſt in the Country, as Politicks and Morality were at *London* and *Whitehall*. A new Scheme of Government was to be contriv'd, and new Methods of Adminiſtration, and new Meaſures of Loyalty ſet up: A Man was not to Conſider or Reflect, on pain of being accounted a *Whigg* or *Trimmer*; Names of Diſtinction of the two Extremes. *Tory* and *Whigg* were maliciouſly contriv'd by way of Reproach; and what was worſe, that he might be ſure to go with the Court-Tide and Stream, the Moderate Character was expoſed as the worſt of all: We were not by any means to reaſon on Government, but 'twas required that we ſhould wink, or be blind, and implicitly ſubmit our Underſtandings to Patriarchal and Arbitrary Doctrines and Examples, to prepare Us for what was to follow. Such were our Kings, ſuch our Miniſters, and ſuch were the People to be. But all theſe Kings of the *Scotch* Line ſeem to have differ'd in their Ideas and Methods of Government. King *James* the Firſt Philoſophiſed upon it; *Charles* the Firſt Reaſon'd on it (with too much *Opiniatretie*), and King *Charles* the Second Banter'd it; and I'm ſure King *James* the Second did not Moralize upon it.

JAMES II.

IF what Sir *William Temple* says of King *Charles* the II^d be true, and he gives good Authority for it, *viz.* "That "the Prince of *Orange* upon Discourse, *&c.* "said to him, That the King (*Charles* II^d) "was (as he had reason to be confi- "dent) in his Heart a Roman Catho- "lick, though he durst not profess it; It will go a great way towards the justification of those Gentlemen, and their Conduct in the *Oxford* Parliament, *&c.* in relation to the past King, and much more the Behaviour of the Nation towards King *James*, of whom there was no doubt of being one, and who dar'd own it at last, though he very meanly prosecuted One upon a *Scandalum Magnatum* for having said so once: For no doubt they both came over as much Papists as they ever were; and if the first dyed such, I can't but believe he had lived one for Thirty Years at least; and they will both stand in need of a very great Dispensation somewhere else, for their Hypocrisy so many Years. If King *Charles* believ'd nothing of the Popish Plot

Plot (as is said) I know not whether it will diminish the Credit of it: But 'tis certain his Successor King *James* abundantly confirm'd its Credibility, even so much as to give a Reputation to the intended Bill of Exclusion; though the Loyalty of the People then ran so high, that they were not willing to part with him without Experience; nor then neither, it seems, by some; vainly imagining, that the Honour of a Popish King could supersede, and take place of his Religion. The Books and Pamphlets of that Season, have sufficiently exposed or demonstrated the Character of this King, and the Principles of that Religion. And 'twas as Evident to any body that would see what he had been doing in his Brother's Reign, as what he did in his own. Whether we conclude his Practice from his Principles, or his Principles from his Practice, there's enough to convince for the past, and to caution for the time to come. If Declarations repeated with so much Solemnity, and broke through with so much Ease, and a Coronation-Oath Discharged and Violated so plainly though with an impertinent Distinction of the Judges to keep up a feeble Countenance of Law: For what

L 4

will not Judges in Commiſſion **during pleaſure** ſay or do? For our Judges are not Sworn as thoſe Judges, whom the Kings of *Egypt* made ſolemnly to take an Oath that they would not do any thing contrary to their Conſcience, (though commanded to it by themſelves.) If the Buſineſs of the *Iriſh* at *Portſmouth*: If the ſending the *Lord Caſtlemain* to *Rome*, and receiving a Nuntio here, which was never ſuffer'd in a Proteſtant Country, nor at Treaties where Proteſtant Miniſters have been: If the Letters from *Liege* to the *Jeſuits* at *Friburg*: If ſending the Lord *Preſton* to *France*, which ſufficiently implies a *French* League, to mention no other Evidence of it; nor the Story of ſending out the Fleet Half-Mann'd: If theſe or any of theſe did not unvail the Deſigns of that King, we ſhall ever be in the Dark, and nothing on this ſide of Dragooning could have open'd their Eyes; they muſt alſo be perſuaded, That the Pope, King *Lewis*, and King *James* were all well-wiſhers to the Proteſtant Religion, and to the Heretick Proſperity of *England*, as by Law Eſtabliſh'd. That inviduous little Management of *Magdalen* College Affair, with Huffing a parcel of poor naked Fellows of a College, for not ſwal-

swallowing Perjury, without a Dispensation, shews his good Nature, equally with his Policy, and sets forth in Epitome his Devout Observation of an Allowance to Church-of-*England* Consciences. The prosecuting the Bishops so Barbarously: *First*, One for refusing to do what was not in his power, by Law, and then the rest for humbly begging to be allowed to have Souls: The turning all the Nobility and Gentry out of all Commissions, Offices, and Places, for pretending to Honour, and refusing to concur in Dissolving the Reformation, was a Master-stroke, that we might be subdued and overrun with *Jesuits* Councels, and *Irish* Courage and Conduct. Some of his Friends are so Hardy to fancy and pretend to say, He could not have introduced Popery, if he had endeavoured it; they should have put in Arbitrary Power too: For what cannot a King do, over a passive People, Disarm'd in Power, and Defective in Notion and Thought? *Cependant les Anglois se doivent souvenir le Massacre* D'Ireland, *&c.* says a late *French* Author; but I forbear to give you any Account from the *French* Refugees. 'Tis true, he could not subdue our Understandings, but he might exercise a fatal Tyranny over our Wills: Besides,

sides, King *James* never tried fair means, which would have went a great way; he went the false way to work upon *Englishmen*: I doubt we are not so much Temptation-proof: And it might, for ought I know, have been a dangerous Experiment, to have trusted the Church with it self so long in an Enemy's Quarter. We see King *James* hath lived a great many Years, enow to have gone a great way with us, with the Assistance of *French* and *Irish*, and such Subjects as were inclinable to be of the King's Religion at Home; and he must have gone as far as he could: No doubt the Nation had been as easily supplied as *Magdalen*-College. But it happen'd very luckily for *England*, that King *James* discover'd his Temper of Spirit a little too soon. We all knew of what force Edicts had been in *Hungary* and *France*, the Copies whereof our Kings had been so apt to follow; and what the Duke of *Savoy* had been doing in the Valleys of *Piedmont*; but we would not believe King *James* was Cruel, was a Persecutor, scarce that he was a Papist, because he had the Art to Conceal and Disguise himself a little, before it was in his power to use the Rod. But presently Father *Petre* shew'd that he would do as much in *England*,

England, as *la Chaise* had done in *France*; and the first was observ'd to be the hottest of the two: And not to aggravate or mince Matters; They must all have done what lay in their power, in Obedience to what their Councils Decree towards the Extirpation of Hereticks. But God be thanked King *James* did not shew himself that Prince of Resolution; at least he fail'd them in one Character, as they would have had him deceiv'd us by another. He was pleased for some Considerations (whether of Fear or Guilt) to leave us abruptly, and we have taken that Advantage of parting with him fairly: And I wish him all the Happiness that is consistent with the Welfare of *England*. Only let us as *Englishmen* remember, That we now have an Act of Parliament of our side, which Asserts the Rights and Liberties of the Subject, and hath Establish'd the Settlement of the Crown; and which incapacitates any Papist, or Person Marrying a Papist, from having and enjoying it; which Act is only Defective in this, That it is not Order'd to be *Read in the Churches twice at least every Year, and upon Penalty of Deprivation*. If such a Law had been made in *Edward* the VIth's Time, it might have sav'd some Blood and Trouble since the Reformation. *WILLIAM*

WILLIAM III.

THE Lord Chancellor *Notttingham* in the Case of the Duke of *Norfolk* and *Charles Howard* Esquire, &c. hath, in my Mind, a notable Expression, *viz.* "Pray let us so Resolve Cases here, "that they may stand with the Reason "of Mankind when they are Debated "abroad." Shall that be Reason here, that is not Reason in any part of the World besides? In truth, we are apt to be peculiarly Artificial in our Thoughts and way of Argument, and our Reasonings are too Municipal. Thus every little Pedant can Settle and Establish the Affairs of Religion and Government, and can Resolve all the great Mysteries of Church and State (as he thinks) in his narrow Study. But if a Man looks Abroad, and takes a general survey of the World, and reflects upon the Universal Notions and Customs of Mankind, his Soul will become more enlarged, and will not determine so Magisterially upon the Principles of any particular Sect or Society.

The

The Case of King *WILLIAM* in it self, is, perhaps, the most Glorious and Generous Cause that hath appeared upon the Stage of Human Actions; yet hath been sullied by dire Representations, by poor-spirited and precarious Arguments, which have been brought in for its support. His Title to the Crown of *Great Britain* stands Firm, and is justifiable upon Natural and Sound foundations of Reason, without Props: But hath been so oddly maintained by the manner of its Defence, that it hath been the Justification only that hath Disgrac'd the Revolution: *Doctrina facit Difficultatem.* We have been running out of the way to fetch in Aids from Art and Learning, whilst Nature presents us with obvious and undefiled Principles of Reason. Thus the King's Accession to the Throne hath been introduced by shuffling between Providential Settlement, Conquest, Desertion, Abdication, and topping Protections of Power; whilst Men of Honour, and People of Honest Plain Understandings, stand Amazed, instead of being Convinced; and hang back when Allegiance comes to be explained, and a Recognition demanded; an Association proposed, frights us as a thing strange and impious; which shews our Allegiance

ance was not rightly founded, but looks like a thing of Fancy, built upon a forc'd and fictitious bottom. All these ungrateful Terms have been ingeniously exposed by M*r* *Johnson*, except only *Abdication*; which, with submission, is also too Artificial; a Word not to be found in the Alphabet of *Spelman*; a Civil Law Term (used almost in Fifty several Senses) and therefore an uncouth Expression of the Common Laws of this Realm to speak in: The Word *Forfaulture* seems to have a plainer Signification to our common Understanding: This, as *Forisfacere, Forisfactum, Forisfactura*; and *Forfacere, Forfactum, Forfactura, &c.* we find in *Spelman*, and it signifies, *Rem suam ex delicto amittere, & sibi quasi extraneum facere, Rem culpâ abdicere, alterique, Puta Regi, Magistratui, Domino abjudicare: Forisfacere pro Delinquere, peccare, transgredi, Injuriam inferre:* LL. Edw. Confess. cap. 32. *ut Codex noster MS. legit, Aliqui stulti & improbi. gratis & nimis consuetè erga vicinos suos foris faciebant.* This agrees with the Sense of King *James* the I*st* his Speech to his Parliament, *viz. A settled King is bound to observe the Paction made to his People by his Laws, in framing his Government agreeable thereunto: And a King Governing in a settled Kingdom,*

leaves

leaves to be a King, *and degenerates into a* Tyrant, *as soon as he leaves off Governing according to the Laws.* In which Case the King's Conscience may speak to him (as the Poor Widow said to *Philip* of *Macedon,*) Either Govern according to your Law, *aut ne sis Rex:* And if a Subject's Conscience may not speak the same thing, King *James's* Words signify nothing. The other Words carry an Odious or suspected Construction in them; the First (in the Convocation-style) implies Guilt, and at best creates but a *Transylvanian* Allegiance; the Second is a Jest, and false in Fact, besides 'tis what the King himself disowns; the Third is an idle Sham, as stated; and the Fourth is also a little strain'd, as I concieve; and we might, for ought I see, as well have call'd it a Cession, especially if King *James* was a Spiritual Person of the Society of Jesuits, as hath been said. But what need we any Term of Art? Let the matter express it self by Periphrasis in its own genuine Phrase. It is fairly stated in the Prince's Declaration: And our Case is no more nor less than this; A King, contrary to his Coronation Oath, dispenses with, and breaks through all the Established Laws of the Land, Invades and Subverts the Rights, Liberties, and Properties of the People, which he Swore
to

to maintain inviolably; and Diſſolves the Conſtitution of Church and State, in an Arbitrary Tyrannical manner; the People therefore in Defence of their Laws, Rights, and Religion, and the neceſſary Preſervation of them, Oppoſe the violent proceedings of ſuch a Prince (I put the Caſe at the worſt) and alſo apply themſelves to a Neighbouring Prince, (who hath an Expectation of a Right to the Crown), and pray in Aid of him to aſſiſt them in the Maintaining and Defending their Legal Rights, together with his own Title to the Succeſſion; who, in his own Words, makes Preparation to Aſſiſt the People againſt the Subverters of their Religion and Laws, and alſo Invites and Requires all Perſons whatſoever, "All the " Peers of the Realm, Spiritual and Tem- " poral, and all Gentlemen, Citizens, and " other Commons of all Ranks, to come " and aſſiſt him in order to the Execution " of this Deſign, againſt all ſuch as ſhall " endeavour to Oppoſe them, to prevent " all thoſe Miſeries which muſt needs fall " upon the Nations being kept under Ar- " bitrary Government and Slavery; and " that all the Violences and Diſorders " which have overturn'd the whole Con- " ſtitution of the *Engliſh* Government, " may be fully Redreſſed in a Free and Le- " gal Parliament, to ſecure the Nation
" from

"from relapsing into the Miseries of Ar-
"bitrary Government any more." Upon which appearance of mutual Defence for Self-preservation, the Conscious King Retires, first leaves his Army, (which no Man I will be bold to say would do without Guilt or Cowardice, and I'm sure a Prince that had been Brave, or acted upon Principles of Honour, would have Fought it out with but Ten Regiments, or with One at his Heels, which was *Richard* the III^d's Case in the first sence, though not in the later) and after leaves the Realm, for Reasons best known to himself (whether Frighted, or not, is not material) upon which, the Prince, together with his Consort, the next Heir (Indisputable) to the Crown, in a full and due Representation of the whole Community and Body of the Kingdom, is and are Declared and Appointed King and Queen.

Now let us see what we have done upon the whole matter, to deserve that harsh Language of the Convocation-Book, produced by Dr *Sherlock*; Whether we have done more, or so much as all other Nations have done in a Case any thing like Ours? Whether we have done more than becomes Good Christians, or Men of Honour? And what it is that stands in our way

way to hinder or bar such an Attempt and Action?

First, Setting aside at present those Texts of St. *Paul* and St. *Peter*, which are the only discouraging Impediments, and which have been sufficiently, as I think, answered and avoided by several Pens: Upon the Law of Nature, no Man, I believe, can pretend to say, here is any Natural Injustice, or Moral Injury done; Certainly Nature and Reason prompt us to Defend Injuries, and to Repel Force; Nature will preserve it self in its Being. No Man will say a King of *England* hath power of Life and Death over his Subjects (We say he hath no Power, other than by the Law of the Land); the Moral, as well as Legal Consequence must be, That we may Defend our Lives against all Assaults; 'tis the same of Liberty and Property; for there is a *Meum* and *Tuum* in all Christian Commonwealths, as Archbishop *Abbot* said before, subject only to the Laws of the Place; therefore I can't defend my self or House against the King Arm'd with Legal Power, as upon a *Cap. Utlagatum*, or upon a Duty due to him, &c. but I may, where I am out of the compass of a Legal Prosecution. If the consequence of Self-defence and Preservation be denied, it's vain trifling to talk of Laws, and

and to value our selves upon Living in a Country where the Measures of Right are ascertain'd, and the Limits of Government and Subjection; the Doctrine of *Passive Obedience*, and the *Bow String*, will be the same, if Laws are only a simple Direction for Information, and not an Obligation. We must owe our Lives, &c. at this rate, to Fortune, not to Justice: But since the Restoration, it's said we are under another Tie, not to take up Arms, by the Extravagant Compliment to King *Charles* the II^d, and the Declaration pursuant to that Act. Be it so; though all Laws made in Extraordinary Heats are not a regular Obligation; but let them take that State-Artificial Obligation into the Bargain; the King Swears too, and this was not designed to let loose the King's Hands, and tie the Subjects; for all Obligations, whether Natural or Artificial, are Reciprocal and Mutual, and always so taken and understood in common Intendment. There can be no other Notion of Justice, Natural, Moral, or Political; and whatever Preference and Advantage is allowed to One above the Other, 'tis an Authority upon Supposition of Care, Protection, and for Order, and centers in the Good of the Community. And, I think, the *Lacedemonians* had a Law to Punish Parents who did not their Duty towards their

their Children. Let us therefore take in the highest Instance of Obedience and Duty from Children to Parents: No Man, I suppose, will pretend now, that a Father may Castrate, Sell, or Kill a Child; the Inference must be, That in any Case of such open Violence, a Son may Resist a Father, in his own necessary Defence and Self-preservation (without offering Reproach, Injury, or Vindictive Force): So in the Case of Lunacy in a Parent, or any fatal Extravagance, no doubt a Son may lay Hands on a Father by way of Restraint, and must take a continued Commanding Care over him, in case of Relapse, &c. This is agreed on all hands to be the severest Tie of Obedience; and therefore Kings are endeavoured to be brought within the Fifth Commandment to make our Chains the faster; not in the mean time considering that they make them looser, by putting an inconsistent double Duty upon us. Thus we are told Religion stands positively in our way, and fetters us with an Absolute Obedience to Kings without Reserve, &c. It seems hard that Religion should weaken our Arm in Defence of it self, and force our Obedience and Submission to Laws and Absolute Power in the same breath: For where there is Absolute Power, there is no Law; and where there are Laws, there is no Absolute Power.

But

But Scripture is to be our Guide; I agree it: But what Authority shall I rely on? Where shall I apply my self for an Interpreter? 'Tis manifest our own Church cannot settle me, that is divided against it self. Some bring Instances from the Old Testament; Others tell us, That is nothing to the purpose, those Kings being by God's Designation, &c. Some tell us, these Texts of *St. Peter* and *St. Paul* oblige us to Passive Obedience on peril of Damnation: And Others as boldly and magisterially inform us, That the New Testament gives no Rules for Submission to Forms of Government, but only Rules of Justice, Order, and Peace; That those Texts are nothing to Our purpose; for the Apostles spoke to those under Heathen Emperors, where *Paganism* was Established by a Law; and that those Texts are to be only Expounded against the *Jews*, who still believed themselves under the Divine Authority, and thought they could not become the Subjects of any other Power. As to the Scripture-Examples, we are Taught by a very great Divine and Bishop, not to rely on them; and he says, Those who place the Obligatory Nature of these Examples from Scripture, must either produce the Moral Nature of those Examples, or else a Rule binding us to follow those Examples, especially when these

these Examples are brought to found a New positive Law Obliging all Christians. Some say in general, the Bible is a Miscellaneous Book, where Dishonest and Time-serving Men may ever, in their loose way, find a Text for their purpose. Sir *Robert Filmer* upon the Dispute of the Form of Powers (for these Texts are sometimes applied to the Form, and sometimes to the Quality of Power) takes Power only in the Singular Number; Powers in the Plural is a damnable Sin; and he will have all Governments but the Patriarchal, to be Illegal and Abominable; but this is so Extravagant, that, I think, none of our Divines pretend to justify him in it; and therefore Others, on the contrary, are of Opinion, That Submit to all Powers, infers, That all Forms of Government are admitted to be good, and do not allow that *Power* in the Singular is to be taken restrictive, and so there is no Authority, if not of God, and the Authorities which are (of God's Institution) are ordered under God. Sir *Robert Filmer*, D*r Hicks*, &c. will have the Legislative Power to be in the King alone. And the First says, all Legislative Powers are Arbitrary; But where is the necessity for that? And D*r Hicks* says also, Only the Laws of Men are God's Ordinances: St. *Paul*, speaking of Authority in general, says,

Ordi-

Ordinance of God. St. *Peter,* of the particular Persons administring Authority, calls it, the *Ordinance of Man*; Sir Robert *Filmer* upon that, *Render unto Cesar, the things that are Cesars, and unto God the things that are God's,* divides all between God and the King, and leaves nothing to the poor Subject; which doth not very well consist with our Saviour's Advice to him, whom he bid *Sell All that he had, and give to the poor,* which grieved the Young Man, for *he had Great possessions.* It seems by this our Saviour implies the Subject had Property, otherwise he could not have Sold it. Thus they make their own Idol.

We see then by the better Opinions of Divines and Learned Men, all Forms of Power are Authentick, with respect to the Laws and Constitutions of Places; *and submit to all Powers,* imports only Obedience according to Law, the Ordinance of Man; *To render unto Cesar,* &c. implies certainly that something was left in him who rendred: It is not said, Give all to *Cesar.* So no Man will controvert the *submitting to every ordinance,* with the Context; for Rulers are a Terror to the Evil, and not to the Good. There never was any King in *Israel,* but had some Engagement and Tye upon him, Formally with God, or by Covenant with Man: To keep the Laws, to judge righteously,

teously, to seek the Good of the People, &c. Besides, the Case of the Apostles is wonderfully different in all respects: As to Property, &c. the Government of the *Roman* Emperors was Absolute (taking it at worst) and therefore Christians, who had no Law on their side, could not resist: (This is said by some, tho' our Saviour does not seem to mean it so); whereas Ours under our Kings is limited and mixt; therefore not the same foundation to apply the Injunctions of Non-resistance from the Apostles. As to Religion, the Apostles came counter to all Laws, and therefore were to submit to them: Not to raise Rebellion on account of a new Religion, which had no foundation in any Law: And the proper Talent and Business of the Apostles was suffering for the sake of the Gospel; therefore impertinent as well as prophane and wicked for them, to think of resisting any Powers. What is this to the maintaining a Religion established by a Law? But this Construction imposed upon Us towards Passive Obedience, is a Conceit against the Opinion of most Learned Men, and also contrary to the Common Practise of the Christian World. *Grotius, Selden,* &c. understand *submission to every ordinance,* to be to the Government, and the Laws thereof: And so in common construction and intendment, those Texts may be taken a Direction from the Apostles to their Missionaries

ries and Correspondents, who were to travel through variety of Governments to pay all Duties and Civil Respects to Kings and Magistrates, and may be satisfied with that particular application of Obedience: They were enjoined not to enquire into the Fundamental Rights of Power, but to take them as they found them, being only Powers of this World, with proper Laws for keeping Mankind in Peace and Order in general, according to the Respective Customs and Constitutions. I believe besides, the Gospel is an Universal Instruction for Obedience to the Laws, on the severest punishment of disobedience to them: 'Twas intended to make them good Subjects, but not Slaves. 'Tis too much to be Passive and Martyrs by whole Nations, with the Laws and Religion bleeding by our Sides. Let's look into the Customs and Usages of other Ages and Places, and enquire into, and examine the Principles and Opinions of Learned Divines on the Occasions of Power, and the Exercise or Abuse of it. If a man should consult the Histories of the first Kings of *France* and *Spain*, both before and since those Nations receiv'd the Light of the Gospel, and the hudled abrupt Succession, besides the very odd Partnerships in Kingdoms; he will find matter but of small Veneration for Titles to Crowns of Old Times, whatever he may fancy is due to the

the Present Establishments: And I doubt we should discover but a faint blind Track of Active Providence in the transferring Kingdoms (as 'tis call'd) but only rather the Effects of a Ludicrous Fortune. Suppose we should be free, and tell the World we have Elected, Made, or Appointed (call it what you will) King *William* King of *Great Britain*, instead of King *James* (without the formality of Deposing, or taking off his Crown or Head, to make a Vacancy, or without the *Ens Rationis* of a Vacancy); it would be no more than what may be justified by Precedents of no Bad Times in other Countries, and our Own too. In *France*, the Instance of *Childerick* degraded, and *Ægidius* or *Gillon*, Master of the *Roman* Militia (who was a Stranger, but in Reputation for Probity and Wisdom) Elected in his stead. It is said, the *French*, according to their Ancient Rights, conferr'd upon *Pepin* (after *Thierry* was stripp'd of his Royalty) the Sovereignty of *Austrasia*: And afterwards *Pepin* his Grandson (Son of *Charles Martel*, and Father of *Charlemain*) by a Parliament assembled was appointed King, although there was One of the *Marovignian* Race remaining, but Young, Stupid, and Witless: And for the Honour of the Church, Pope *Zachary* confirm'd him: Upon which, in another Parliament at *Reymes*, they degraded

Chil-

Childerick, and Elected *Pepin*: And the Archbishop of *Mentz*, *Boniface*, declared to them the Validity of the Pope's Answer. And after, at the Assembly at *Carbonnac*, the *Austrasian* Lords and Estates acknowledged *Charlemain* their King. They might do, says the History, this, and if he had not had That Right, he had been an Usurper, for the Children of *Charlemain* were living: *Hugh Capet*'s best, if not only Title, was Election: For *Charles* Duke of *Lorrain* was of the *Carolovinian* Race, and Heir, but, as is said, of little merit.

In *Spain* the *Visigoths* (about 1200 years since) made and unmade their Kings as they pleas'd. I suppose 'twill not be said They were the worse Christians for being nearer the time of our Saviour and his Apostles.

So it was in *Denmark* too, till they lately changed from Elective to Hereditary, from a Limited to an Absolute Government; and so, for ought we know, it may again, when that Arbitrary Power hath had its full swing.

To look back here at home; formerly it was so. And I know not why we may not be permitted to go upwards as far as we please, since those on t'other side think fit to go backward to *Henry* the Third for the

begin-

beginning, as they say, of our Constitution. *Egbert* the First, sole *Saxon* King, upon the Report of the Death of *Britric*, with great speed returned out of *France*, where, during the time of his abode, he had serv'd with good Commendation in the Wars under *Charles the Great*; by means whereof, his Reputation encreasing amongst his own Countrymen, he was thought worthy of the Government before he obtained it: And *Ethelwolf* a Monk, a Deacon, and a Bishop, yet Elected King, because they could not find a fitter Person for the Crown. *Edwin* by his Miscarriage turn'd his Subjects Hearts, and the *Mercians* and *Northumbrians* revolted, and swore Fealty to his Younger Brother *Edgar*. The *Danish* Kings were approved by the Lords during their short time of Reign here: *Edward the Confessor* by general Consent was admitted King: *Harold* chose himself, and ravish'd a Crown, and he fared accordingly for his Intrusion without the Consent of the People. All that is intended by this short Account, is, only to shew, That Succession was not always esteemed so Sacred; and that Non-Resistance hath not been so stanch'd a Doctrine always, as some now would pretend.

To come nearer to our present Case, Let's see the Opinion of Councels and Divines, and perhaps we shall not need to be much out

out of Countenance for affifting the Prince of *Orange* in the Vindication of our Civil Rights and Religion, and I believe the Church of *England* will ftand by Us: And Divines of great Reputation gave their Judgment for Subjects defending themfelves againft their Princes in Cafes not near fo ftrong as Ours.

Queen *Elizabeth* gave Countenance and Aid to the Revolt of the *Low-Countries*, or Rebellion, as it is call'd, againft the King of *Spain*; and did it by Advice of Learned and Religious Divines, as Dr. *Bancroft*, &c. And 'twas for the fake of Religion: Queen *Elizabeth* alfo affifted the Proteftants in *Scotland* againft the *French* Faction: *Cambden* fays, fhe had a Confultation about that Matter; and although it was urged, That it was of Ill Example to patronife another Prince's Subjects in Commotion; yet it feem'd to be an Impious thing to be wanting to them of the fame Religion.

Bifhop *Bilfon* juftifies the Defence which the *French* and *Dutch* made, on fuppofition that it was for the Maintenance of the Laws.

If we look into the Affair of the King of *Bohemia*, or Prince *Palatine*, we find (tho King *James* was backward, *i.e.* fearful, and
had

had not Courage when the War broke out in *Germany*) the Sense of the Archbishop, in his Letter to Sir *Robert Naunton*, Secretary of State, when he advised the King to send Aid against the Emperor's Attempts of introducing Popery and Arbitrary Power; he encourages the Prince *Palatine* as King of *Bohemia* by Election, in the matter for propagation of the Gospel, and to protect the Oppress'd, and declares for his own part, He did not dare but give Advice to follow where God leads; apprehending the Work of God in This, and That of *Hungary*; and that he was satisfied in Conscience that the *Bohemians* had a Just Cause, *&c.*

King *Charles* the First, who appeared to be of as Scrupulous a Judgment in the Point as any, By the Advice of Archbishop *Laud*, not only assisted the King of *Denmark* (who assisted others) against the House of *Austria*, to keep the King of *Spain* from overrunning the Western part of *Christendom*, and sent Forces and Supplies for the Cause of Religion; as his Reasons are emphatically express'd in the Declaration: But also some time after published a Declaration of War against *France*, chiefly on Account of that King's Protestant Subjects, for Violation of Edicts, and Breach of Articles and Contracts with them. Whereas Contracts and Articles at other times with Us have, by some, been

been pronounced Prophane Absurdities, &c.

The Revolt of *Catalonia* hath had its due Representation here as well as elsewhere: The only Reason for their taking up Arms, was, in plain Terms, to rid themselves of their Oppressors, which the Nobility said was their Duty; and to preserve their Ancient Form of Government from the Encroachments of the King of *Spain*, who Oppress'd Rich and Poor by Arbitrary Taxations; Religion was no Ingredient in their Rebellion: Their Acclamations were, *Long live the new King D'Juan de Braganza, and let them dye that govern ill*. His Accession to the Crown of *Portugal* was Congratulated and Countenanced by all the Kingdoms and States in *Europe* upon the Return of his *Manifesto's*; (only the Emperor, whose Interest it was, condemn'd it) the Pope himself did not Resent it. And they congratulated him upon the Merits, as well as Success of the Attempt.

Where then is this Ambitious Prince? Where is that Wicked and Ungodly People, as they call Us? We have done no more than what hath been done upon a Godly Consideration in like Cases; nay not so much, and our Case goes farther; for these had only Edicts and Acts of Grace to maintain; We defend our Religion Establish'd by the Laws of the Land. This

This Family of the *Naſſaus* have the hardeſt Meaſure under the Sun; To be ſtiled Daring and Ambitious Spirits, and to have Damnation thus Entailed upon them, only for undertaking the Cauſe of the Oppreſs'd, and Reſcuing Abus'd Innocence from the Tyranny of Arbitrary and Barbarous Power.

Why then are the Gentlemen of the Church of *England* ſo reſty upon this Revolution? There is ſcarce any Reaſon to be imagined, unleſs it be for thoſe which they bring themſelves; ſuch as the Convocation-Settlement, Conqueſt, *&c*. If we ſhould enquire into their Opinions, and variety of Principles, I doubt we ſhall find them ſo Un-uniform, that we ſhall never ground any fixt Authority upon them in this Point, or any other. Tho it ſeems but an Ungrateful Task to expoſe their Contradictions and Contrarieties in all Ages: But if they have differ'd amongſt themſelves in their Doctrines and Notions of Obedience, or Reſiſtance, and the Settlement of Crowns, I hope they will give Us leave in Equal Authorities to chuſe which we will follow: In truth, he who will be at the pains to examine their Writings, *i. e.* their General Councels themſelves, even from the firſt Four, to the Laſt, I'm ſorry to ſay it, will, I be-

I believe, find but a Sandy Foundation to fix his Conscience or Judgment in Articles of Faith. What have they been doing with the Trinity of late? What have they not been doing to get the Government into the Church-Conusance by way of Success and Providence? Tho I would have this Government setled to satisfy and please every one in their own way, if it were possible, for Men have different Ideas of things: Yet I'am unwilling the Government should be trick'd and impos'd upon: And that Men should advance their own Stations and Interest, by publishing and mis-applying Notions which expose the Church and King both: I must confess, I think Dr. S—— Reasons for the Government have been the greatest against it with all Men of Reason and Honour, and have hindred many from coming into it. What stuff have we produced in a Convocation-Book! the greatest Affront to a King and People that was ever offer'd with a *salvo* to the Church. It is said, "Providence may actually, and God will, "when he sees fit, and can serve the Ends of "his Providence, set up Kings without any "Regard to Legal Right, or Human Laws; "and when they are thus set up, they are "invested with God's Authority, which "must be obey'd, and this supersedes all Le- "gal Disputes of Right, and our old Oaths "and our old Allegiance are at an end: For

"when

"when God transfers Kingdom
"set over Us a New King (and
"and requires our Obedience
"King, he necessarily transfers
"ance, &c. And the Authority
"ten and wrested from the Tr
"ful Possessor, being always G
"ty, and therefore receiving
"ment from the Wickedness
"have it, is ever, when any A
"truly setled, to be obeyed :
(tho as with a supposing) to
by this, That the Nobility ar
this Nation have been banter
mighty with Prayers and Pr
while, whereas both Prince and
All of Us, should have been
selves in Sackcloth and Ashe
Pennance for our Rebellion and
I shall not trouble a Serious T
this Convocation-Book, or the
it; enough hath been said abou
Doctor already. King *James* I.
to Dr. *Abbot*, shews his Resen
Proceedings of that Convocati
will produce another Convoca
how the former hath setled
ment : The first was in the t
the First, the other in *James*
Now you shall see the Judg
mous University of *Oxon*:
Convocation reflecting (as t

upon certain Pernicious Books, and Damnable Doctrines, (*viz* amongst others, Proposition 10. "That Possession and Strength "give a Right to Government; and Success in a Cause or Enterprize proclaims it "to be Lawful and Just; *(Nota)* To pursue it, Is to comply with the Will of God, "because it is to follow the Conduct of his "Providence: *Hobbes, Owen, Baxter, Jenkins,* &c. And Proposition 15. "If a People, who by Oath and Duty are obliged to a Sovereign, shall sinfully Dispossess him, and, contrary to their Covenant, chuse and covenant with another, they may be obliged by their Latter Covenant, notwithstanding their "Former; *Baxter,* H. C. &c.) by their Judgment and Decree, *Ann.* 1683. pronounced these, amongst many other such like Propositions, Heretical; and Decreed, Judged, and Declared them to be False, Seditious, and Impious, Blasphemous and Infamous to Christian Religion, and destructive of all Government in Church and State: What a Blessed Establishment is here! What an Honourable Title hath the King! in what a Condition is the Subject! Thus we see how unsafe 'tis to imply or suppose a Providential Usurper, or King *de facto*, which is all one; and then to secure him by Arguments out of the Clouds. So 'tis of a Forcible Usurper, or King *de facto*,

t'other

t'other way, to Establish him with a Providential Success, as Conqueror, without Right: As if we come to measure the Mysteries of Providence by our narrow Comprehensions and Rules, and tack it to every Success, we shall make a very odd Business of it, and put Providence upon very Irreverent Offices. We know how That, and Scripture hath been interpreted upon other Occasions: In less than half a Century, upon a Certain Revolution, One Side said, God shewd his Indignation in Thunder and Lightning: T'other, That he Congratulated the Success with his Guns and Fireworks from above. *Plato* in his time said, Lawyers and Physicians were the Pest of a Country: Would he not have added, Divines also; had he lived in some other Ages?

When these Gentlemen were upon their Providential Disposal and Settlement of Kingdoms, They might as justly have brought some Instances from Scripture, which would have been for the Honour of the Revolution Where God vouchsaf'd his Assistance to a good Cause for a Blessing to a People (as well as always for a Curse to a Bad and Sinful Nation) Instances which comply and would have stood with the Ordinary Rules of Morality and Human Justice. As the Case of *Solomon* and his Son, between

between *Hezekiah* and *Josiah*, and the succeeding Tyrants, and Wicked Princes. Also in the Case of *Rehoboam*, where God seems to give a Countenance to the Revolt of the Ten Tribes, and assist against his Tyranny and Oppression; for God says, 'twas his doing there also. *David* seems to agree with this: He sufficiently differences his Expressions, according to the Characters of Princes and Rulers, as good or bad: He tells us the Fate of wicked ones, not by executing upon them God's immediate personal Judgments, or by the visible Hand of Providence; but by Human Mediums of interposing Power to restrain them, &c. by the Favour of God's Assistance in an Ordinary Course of Providential Justice: The Prophets did not preach Passive Obedience to the Idolatrous Kings of *Israel* and *Judah*, but inveigh'd against them. Did not *David* and his Adherents resist *Saul*, though he spared his Person: (I do not pretend to plead for a Vindictive Account against the Person of Kings) And the Story of *Manasses* methinks seems something toward ours: He Set up, Repaired, Adorn'd, and Furnish'd the Altars, Temples, and High Places in which the Devil was by the Heathen Worshipp'd, forgetting the Piety of his Father, and most abominably burnt his Sons for a Sacrifice to the Devil, *Moloch*,

Moloch, and shed so much innocent Blood, that 'tis said, *Jerusalem* was replenish'd therewith. And when after all, he was reprehended by the Reverend Prophet *Esai*, he caus'd him to be Saw'd asunder with a Wooden Saw. Therefore for his Sins, the Lord brought upon him the Captains of the Host of the Kings of *Ashur*, who took *Manasses*, and put him in Fetters, and bound him in Chains, and carried him to *Babel*, where, after he had lain Twenty Years as a Captive, despoiled of all Honour and Hopes of doing Mischief, God inspir'd him with Repentance, and afterwards mov'd the *Assyrians* Heart to deliver him; after which he forgot his Impieties and Villanies, detested his Idolatry, cast down the Idols of his own Erection, repaired *Jerusalem*, and at last Dyed in a Religious Peace. But 'tis not my Province to apply Scripture, only to my self: And I know not what Commission They have so familiarly to determine the Councils of the Almighty. 'Tis true, as St. *Augustin* says, "Nothing "is sensibly and visibly done in the World, "which cometh not from the Interior and "Invisible Cabinet of God, whether it "be commanded or permitted; though some will not allow a permissive Providence, yet the Psalmist says, *Oh God! How profound are thy thoughts! and how unsearchable*

searchable to the ignorant and foolish? Yet Man must be presently making Inferences. Providence is said to take care of the most minute Creatures, as well as the greatest. And these great Texts and Stories of Prerogative and Supremacy, with Complement to each other, are only taken notice of; whilst Others as positive lye dormant; as, *Resist not evil*; *Turn t'other Cheek*; and about giving the Cloak also. These might do mischief, and the Wicked of the World might take Advantage by returning them upon the Exhorters. The Practice of the World runs otherwise, and the Prospect is too Melancholy, where there is no Sunshine in the Landscape.

If then neither the Historical part of the Old Testament, nor the Doctrinal parts of the New, nor the certain Authority of Councils or Convocations, nor the Extrajudicial Opinions of Divines, do unanimously evince our Duty of blind Obedience, or Non-resistance, under a total subversion of a Constitution in Church and State, and the Practice of the Christian World, in all places is counter to it; Why are these Gentlemen so severe upon us, and so resty themselves? Lay the Scene in *Holland*, *Germany*, *France*, (where a Holy League is no News) or *Portugal*, &c. Resistance is an Orthodox Doctrine;

Doctrine; but put the Case at Home, it must be Heretical, and no less than Damnation. Why must *English*-men be the only Cullyes of *Europe*, and have their hands ti'd? Although the Church of *England* does not pretend to follow the Doctrines of the Church of *Rome*; yet I verily believe they never thought to betray their own Church to that, by setting up a contrary Doctrine. *Suarez de Legibus* acquaints us with the Popish Doctrine, expresly in this Case, *viz.* "That Heathen "Kings can't be depriv'd of their power "by War, unless they abuse it, to the In- "jury of Christian Religion, or the Destru- "ction of the Faithful that are under them, "as is the constant Opinion of Divines, meaning of the Church of *Rome*. And again, If Infidels have the Faithful for their Subjects, and would turn them from the Faith or Obedience of the Church, then the Church hath just cause of War against them: But for Heretick Princes, he says, the Church hath Direct power over them, and may deprive them in punishment of their Infidelity or Heresy. This we saw verified in Queen *Elizabeth*, and she by Advice of her Divines, in preservation of Church, turn'd the Tables upon them. I do not believe any of our Divines are so passive, to betray their Church, and yield to the Pope, or any one commission'd by him, their

Dig-

Dignities and Revenues, though they Deliver over the Nobility and Gentry to Damnation, for preserving them in possession of them. I mean they who have taken the Oaths to the Government, as a King *de facto*, for I believe the Others who are not come in, are more charitable; for I confess I have an Honourable pity for them, and value them never the less for sticking to something, though they are unfortunate, and differ from me in Judgment. But besides the Business of Religion, the Papists ought not to be angry with us, for Deposing or Removing a King; they are uneasy as soon as others, and do not take the Passive Doctrine to be any Restraint upon them, even in the ill Administration of a Popish King; Witness that Story of the King of *Spain* in *Portugal*, and the Advance of the Duke of *Braganza*. And here at home to look back and instance only in *Edward* the II^d, who, as the History says, being govern'd by *Gaveston* and the *Spencers*, murder'd his Uncle *Thomas* Earl of *Lancaster*, and numbers of Great men, The People, the Popish People, rose against him, Imprison'd him, and a full Repesentative of the Nation, in a solemn manner renounced their Allegiance to him; but told him withal, they would suffer his Son *Edward* to succeed, which was a favour, it seems, in those Times. Therefore, I think, the Papists, whether they consider their

their Doctrine or their Practice, can't hit us in the Teeth justly: Their only Grievance is, That the Person is mistaken, and doth not prove for their turn. And I do not doubt, notwithstanding Dr. *Sherlock*'s Settlement, they would endeavour to remove King *William*, for King *James*, or any other Popish King again: And I can't blame them for it, for 'tis their Principle; but as Gentlemen they ought to give us leave to enjoy our fancy too. And so to look into our own Church-men, who would seem to mince the matter, either in their Principles or Practice; They tell us a Story of *Licinius* and *Constantine*, and endeavour to parallel the first with King *James* II^d, and justify the latter for making War upon him, by whom they intimate King *William*; but they manage it so scurvily, on and off, that one knows not where to have them; they would, and they would not, as if they were asham'd of their Passive Doctrine, and yet asham'd to quit it. The Bishop of *A.* allows a Foreign Prince to make War upon Another, who prosecutes his Subjects for Religion, if the Religion be his that makes War, for that reason; and what is this more than hath been said before? But *Puffendorf* speaks boldly, and allows also Subjects to use an Absolute Prince as an Enemy, if he discovers an Hostile Mind towards them. We keep a Clutter withour filial Obedience to the Patriarchal Power, &c. But *Puffendorf* grounds even the Paternal Power over Children upon their presum'd Consent, and says, 'tis admitted, Sons may, when they come of Age, chuse whether they will be under their Father's Government, or not. And here (by way of Parenthesis,) a Man might raise an unlucky Dispute; Whether there be any Government Legal and Rightful, but what is only obtain'd by Consent? For if this be true, it will go a great way in the Argument, even of their Patriarchal Power, which for this reason cannot be Absolute, and no Other way can give any Right at all; for Conquest is but an overgrown Trespass upon the Possession and Right of another: And if there be no Government, but by Consent of the Governed, whether the People's Consent will carry a Government farther without a subsequent and continued Approbation? And the Consequence of that, when we Swear Allegiance to a King, be not that it is to be understood no farther than he governs by Law; and that our Allegiance is due to Law, not to the person of a King? Whether these Considerations may not be offer'd with as good a Colour, as some others have been? Whether Kings do not mean this, when the consent of the People is ask'd? Or whether they mean nothing? Whether 'tis not understood by by the consent, &c.? We might also enquire, how our Gentlemen came to be wiser and more scrupulous in their Allegiance than their Forefathers? And what Titles *William* the II^d, *Henry* I^st, *K. John, K. Stephen, Henry* IVth, V^th, VIth, and VIIth had, if not by Consent? We might farther ask them, If this Patriarchal, Despotick, Absolute Power be the Right of Kings, and Non-Resistance is not Lawful upon any occasion whatsoever, Why they are not Unanimous in their Doctrine? And what Lay-men are to do when there is a Schism in the Church? But these may be thought invidious Queries?

But what if these Passive-Gentlemen are not consistent with themselves? 'Tis plain, our Divines here were not so stiff to the first Motions of the Prince's Attempts for our Rescue. He himself tells us, that Several of the Lords Spiritual as as Temporal were in the Inviting of him over; and the Dissenting Archbishop, who thought fit to draw back afterwards, was pleased to Countenance his coming to *London*, and to assist with his Counsels. He was willing to be in the *Sanhedrim* upon the Vacancy; which by his favour was as far from being Passive, as Harnessing and Equipping,

&c.

&c. and several Noblemen with their Chaplains at their Elbows agreed upon the first Overtures against King *James*, who only differ'd after in the Form of Administration, and supplying the Power. There were those who would have been contented and satisfied with a Regency, which by the by was as much against the late Notions of Loyalty; and 'twas once taught, that it was as Damnable to put any Restraint upon a King, or Fetter his Prerogative, or to limit the Measures of our Obedience, as to cancel and throw them off.

If then there be no steady Obstruction in our way, no Irrefragable Arguments, but what are Overturn'd or Embarrass'd; Why may we not throw off the Mask, and declare our selves frankly and sincerely? And talk as becomes Gentlemen or Free-born Creatures, of Reason, and tell the World, That King *James* was no longer fit to be entrusted with the Government; That he could give no Adequate Security for his Administration: That it was no more in his Power, than his Will, to Rule according to Law: That it could not be therefore safe to Re-admit him on any Terms, because he would not be restrain'd by any Qualifications. In short, That King *James*'s Character and Administration are inconsistent and incompatible with
the

the Laws of this Realm ; and that therefore it was neceſſary, abſolutely neceſſary, That the Government ſhould be ſupplied, and ſome Other Perſon admitted and placed in the Throne, from, and by whom might be aſſur'd he would Obſerve and Maintain the Conſtitution in Church and State : And that for theſe Reaſons, we have admitted King *William* to the Crown, allow'd him to take the Goverment as King of *England* , and conſented to transfer our Allegiance to him ; and have Recognized, Acknowledged, and Declared His Majeſty, (he having accepted the Crown and Royal Dignity) To be of Right, and by the Laws of this Realm, our Sovereign Lord and King, of *England, France,* and *Ireland,* and the Dominions thereunto belonging, *&c.*

If our Principles are juſt, the Conſequence muſt be ſo too. If the Premiſes be true, the Concluſion is warrantable. *Montaign* ſays, Authority is not given in favour of the Magiſtrate, but of the People : And 'tis the general Opinion, That Government was made for them, whether originally it were made by them, or not. All the reſpective Schemes of it are contrived to provide for the Welfare of the Community ; and the Laws and Conſtitutions of Power are

the

the Measures of Submission to it. Thus the Notions of Providence and Human Right may be understood, and consist in Human Understanding. Kings and Subjects may know their Duties; Kings may preserve their Rights so long as they continue to be (Rational) Men; and Man may preserve his Native Honour in the Character of his first Creation, as he was made after God's Image also.

Thus I hope this Present King may at last rest in Peace, being setled by such a **Recognition**, and guarded by an **Association** in Parliament. Though 'tis hard to imagine how the Voluntary one came to be boggled at, after such a Declared Right in Parliament before, and Oaths of Allegiance taken to it.

And long may He live to Assert the Rights of the People; To administer Justice, and to retrieve the Honour of *Great Britain*, by vindicating it from the Encroachments suffer'd (not to say consented to) in the late Reigns.

F I N I S.

CORRIGENDA.

PAge 3. Line 16. read *we are.* p. 6. l. 2. r. *off.* p. 8. l. penult. for *affecting*, r. *offering at.* p. 18. l. 17. r. *Sir Henry Spelman.* p. 22. l. 8. r. *Aristotle.* p. 31. l. 15. r. *Government* p. 35. l. 4. r. *they.* p. 116. l. 8. r. *to make War.* p. 118. l. 5. r. *n'avoit.* p. 123. l. 6. r. *ever governed.* p. 137. l. penult. r. *souffers.* p. 152. l. 27. r. *Revenue.* p. 153. l. ay. r. *Opiniatrete.* p. 160. l. 5. r. *Noble.* id. l. 24. r. *and he,* p. 161. l. 5 r. *dir m.* p. 180. l. 28. for *i, e, r, and even,*

www.ingramcontent.com/pod-product-compliance
Lightning Source LLC
Chambersburg PA
CBHW020907230426
43666CB00008B/1342